Diane Wakoski

Diane Wakoski
A Descriptive Bibliography

by

Robert Newton

American Poetry Contemporary Bibliography Series, No. 1

McFarland & Company, Inc., Publishers
Jefferson, North Carolina, and London

PHOTOGRAPHS BY
JUSTIN KESTENBAUM
AND ROBERT TURNEY

Frontispiece: Diane Wakoski, 1977. Photograph by Robert Turney.

Library of Congress Cataloguing-in-Publication Data

Newton, Robert.
  Diane Wakoski : a descriptive bibliography.

  (American poetry contemporary bibliography series ;
no. 1)
  Includes index.
  1. Wakoski, Diane—Bibliography.   I. Title.
II. Series.
Z8947.34.N48   1987   016.811'54   87-43065
[PS3573.A42]

ISBN 0-89950-297-0 (acid-free natural paper) 

Printed in the United States of America.

McFarland   Box 611   Jefferson NC 28640

This is for Gina

Contents

Preface

Diane Wakoski published her early poems, as one critic complained, in "places so obscure that neither moth nor rust has heard of them." One of those magazines has a photograph of the poet on its cover. She is pointing a gun at the camera or, as it seems, at her readers. The poems were aggressive too. Wakoski made startling confessions, fussed with the feminists, and took George Washington as a lover ("Love my country; love George," she explained). Now her bibliography fills a volume.

A writer wants to stay alive, past his lifetime, in the memory of the world. So he gives his poems of confession, contrition, joy and melancholy to the world, and may be famous. "His work is taken from him by the community," Otto Rank said, "as the child is taken from its parents, and in place of it he receives his title to fame, rewarded like a mother by a state hungry for soldiers."

The purpose of the bibliographer must seem related to the writer's motive: He wants to save the writer's work from time. But the bibliographer has no fame to award. He is a maker of lists, and his lists are for the uses of others. A bibliography is an account book of a career of work, done for memory's sake, and in its entries is the record of a life exchanged for poetry, a life renounced in favor of creation.

The first entries in this book, with the letter A preceding an entry number, are for books, pamphlets, broadsides, recordings, and postcards by Diane Wakoski. These entries contain a quasi-facsimile of the title page, and information on the collation, pagination, binding, dust jacket, publication, and contents of the work. Section B describes publications which Diane Wakoski has coauthored. Section C lists the author's publications in periodicals, Section D her appearances in anthologies, Section E her poems translated into other languages, and Section F her published interviews. The appendix lists reviews and criticism of her work.

I have had the use of bibliographies by G.P. Lepper, Walter Hamady, and others. I have kept at hand the excellent bibliography of the Black Sparrow Press by Bradford Morrow and Seamus Cooney. But I have examined each publication myself, almost without exception, and could not have done so if the librarians, archivists, correspondents, publishers, and collectors I bothered had been unkind. Instead, they were benevolent and patient, for no reward except my gratitude.

Clint Colby, Lou Hibe, Mary O'Neil, and Lynn D'Antonio made a week at the Special Collections Library of the University of Arizona as pleasant as could be. Ms. Barbara Richards, of the Rare Books Department of the University of Wisconsin, Madison, has been very good at finding the most obscure publications, and very good to me. Walter Hamady, of the Perishable Press, has been delightful.

I am greatly in debt to Professor Kirk Jones, of the library of Southwestern Oregon Community College, who mounted vast searches, all over the country, for whatever odd thing I requested, and accomplished this from the fastness of the Oregon woods, where we live. He is very competent. He is also the kindest man I have ever met.

I want to thank Diane Wakoski for her great kindness, and her husband, Robert Turney, for his. Having a bibliographer rummage through all the books and papers in your house requires a special courage. They have been unfailingly helpful for more than a year.

I must also thank my wife, Virginia Sutherland, for everything.

Chronology

<table>
<tr><td>1937</td><td>Born August 3 in Whittier, California</td></tr>
<tr><td>1955</td><td>Enters Fullerton Junior College, Fullerton, California</td></tr>
<tr><td>1956</td><td>Enters University of California at Berkeley</td></tr>
<tr><td>1958</td><td>Publishes poems, "Shadows at Stone Henge" and "Translates: Stray Dargon, Nevertheless Blue," in Occident, a student literary magazine</td></tr>
<tr><td>1959</td><td>"First real publication," "Poem," in Coastlines</td></tr>
<tr><td>1960</td><td>Receives B.A. degree</td></tr>
<tr><td>1962</td><td>Four Young Lady Poets
Coins & Coffins</td></tr>
<tr><td>1963</td><td>Teaches at Junior High School 22, Manhattan, 1963–1966</td></tr>
<tr><td>1966</td><td>Discrepancies and Apparitions</td></tr>
<tr><td>1967</td><td>The George Washington Poems</td></tr>
<tr><td>1968</td><td>Greed, Parts 1 and 2
Inside the Blood Factory</td></tr>
<tr><td>1969</td><td>Greed, Parts 3 and 4</td></tr>
<tr><td>1970</td><td>The Magellanic Clouds</td></tr>
<tr><td>1971</td><td>Greed, Parts 5–7
The Motorcycle Betrayal Poems</td></tr>
<tr><td>1972</td><td>Receives Guggenheim Fellowship
Visiting writer, University of Virginia
Smudging</td></tr>
<tr><td>1973</td><td>Greed, Parts 8, 9, 11
Dancing on the Grave of a Son of a Bitch</td></tr>
<tr><td>1974</td><td>Trilogy</td></tr>
</table>

1975   Begins teaching at Michigan State University as Writer in
            Residence
            Virtuoso Literature for Two and Four Hands

1976   Professor of English, Michigan State University
            Waiting for the King of Spain

1978   *The Man Who Shook Hands*

1980   *Cap of Darkness*
            Toward a New Poetry

1982   *The Magician's Feastletters*

1984   *The Collected Greed, Parts 1–13*

1985   *Why My Mother Likes Liberace*

1986   *The Rings of Saturn*

A. Books, Pamphlets, Broadsides

A1   Justice Is Reason Enough   1959

[in black:] JUSTICE IS REASON ENOUGH / BY / DIANE WAKOSKI / FIRST PRIZE / UNIVERSITY OF CALIFORNIA AT BERKELEY / JUNE, 1959 / EMILY CHAMBERLAIN COOK PRIZE IN POETRY / ESTABLISHED BY PROFESSOR ALBERT S COOK / OF YALE UNIVERSITY, IN COMMEMORATION OF / HIS DECEASED WIFE, FORMERLY EMILY CHAM* / BERLAIN OF BERKELEY, CALIFORNIA

Collation: Mimeographed typescript; pp. [1–2]; 8 1/2" × 11".

Pagination: p. [1] title page, p. [2] text.

Publication: 50 copies mimeographed by the author, June 1959, in Berkeley, California.

Contents: "Justice Is Reason Enough."

Note: According to DW, this is "the poet's first true 'publication.'" The rules of the Emily Chamberlain Cook poetry contest required the poet to publish her own poem: "The amount of the prize shall be paid to the successful contestant only after he shall have delivered to the University Librarian fifty copies of his poem, printed at his own expense in a form satisfactory to the Academic Council."

A2   Coins & Coffins   1962

(See photos pages 4 and 5.)

[in black:] COINS / & / COFFINS / Diane Wakoski / HAWK'S WELL PRESS

Collation: pp. [1–6] 7–35 [36]; 7 1/2" × 4 1/2"; printed on wove paper.

Dust jacket of Coins & Coffins.

Title page of Coins & Coffins.

Pagination: p. [1] half-title, p. [2] blank, p. [3] title page, p. [4] copyright, acknowledgments, p. [5] contents, p. [6] dedication, "THIS BOOK IS DEDICATED TO LA MONTE," pp. 7–35 text, p. [36] blank.

Binding: Issued in white paper wrappers. Front cover: [in black:] Diane Wakoski / [black rectangle] / COINS & COFFINS / [black rectangle and, at right, publishers's device]. On left of cover, reading upward: [device] HAWK'S WELL PRESS. On spine, reading downward: [in black:] DIANE WAKOSKI / COINS & COFFINS / HAWK'S WELL PRESS. Back cover reproduces front cover, right to left. Front flap: publisher's statement. Back flap: publications by Hawk's Well Press.

Publication: Published by the Hawk's Well Press, New York, in 1962 at $1.00.

Contents: 7 "Tour," 9 "Dark Windows," 11 "Dialogue," 13 "Justice Is Reason Enough," 14 "Elizabeth and the Golden Oranges," 16 "After Looking at a Painting of the Crucifixion by an Unknown Master of the 14th Century," 18 "Love Poem," 19 "From a Girl in a Mental Institution," 22 "I Am Afraid for the Roses," 23 "Van Gogh: Blue Picture," 25 "To the Lion," 27 "The Few Silver Scales," 28 "And This Is the Way the World Ends: Never," 30 "Cock

Fight under the Magnolias," 31 "Poem to the Man on My Fire Escape," 33 "Coins and Coffins under My Bed."

Note: According to DW, the first printing was of 500 copies.

A3   Discrepancies and Apparitions   1966

(*See photos pages 7 and 8.*)

[in black:] Discrepancies / and Apparitions / by Diane Wakoski / Doubleday & Company, Inc., Garden City, New York, 1966

Collation: pp. [1–10] 11–95 [96]; 8 1/2″ × 5 1/2″; printed on wove paper.

Pagination: p. [1] half-title, p. [2] blank, p. [3] title page, p. [4] copyright and acknowledgments, p. [5] dedication, "This book is for Shapard," p. [6] blank, pp. [7–8] contents, p. [9] half-title, p. [10] blank, pp. 11–95 text, p. [96] blank.

Binding: Black cloth over boards. Stamped in gold on spine, reading downward: Diane Wakoski [device] DISCREPANCIES AND APPARITIONS [device] DOUBLEDAY. Flyleaves are yellow and white (verso).

Dust jacket: Issued in white dust jacket. Front: [in black:] A collection of poems / [in black, distorted print:] Discrepancies / and Apparitions / [in brown, distorted print:] Diane Wakoski. Front flap: note on DW. Back flap: note on DW and quotation from contents. Spine, reading downward: [in black, distorted print:] Discrepancies and Apparitions Diane Wakoski [in black:] Doubleday.

Publication: Published by Doubleday, Garden City, New York, in 1966 at $2.95.

Contents: 11 "Follow That Stagecoach," 14 "Picture of a Girl Drawn in Black and White," 16 "Rock," 17 "Incident of Cherries and Peaches," 20 "Icing the Trains," 22 "From A Go to B, if You Can Find It," 23 "Belly Dancer," 25 "Italian Woman," 26 "Medieval Tapestry and Questions," 28 "The Realization of Difference," 30 "Discrepancies," 38 "Apricot Poem," 40 "All Glitter Is Not Gold," 42 "Letter to the West," 43 "Absence," 46 "Sleep," 47 "Violence," 48 "Midas," 49 "The Oedipus Within," 51 "Scale," 53 "Apparitions Are Not Singular Occurrences," 55 "The First Day," 56 "The Five Dreams of Jennifer Snow and Her Testament," 63 "Winter Apples," 64 "Two Scenes from 'The Tenuous Connection of Dreams,'" 66 "Inside Out," 67 "The Man Who

A collection of poems

Discrepancies and Apparitions

Diane Wakoski

Dust jacket of Discrepancies and Apparitions.

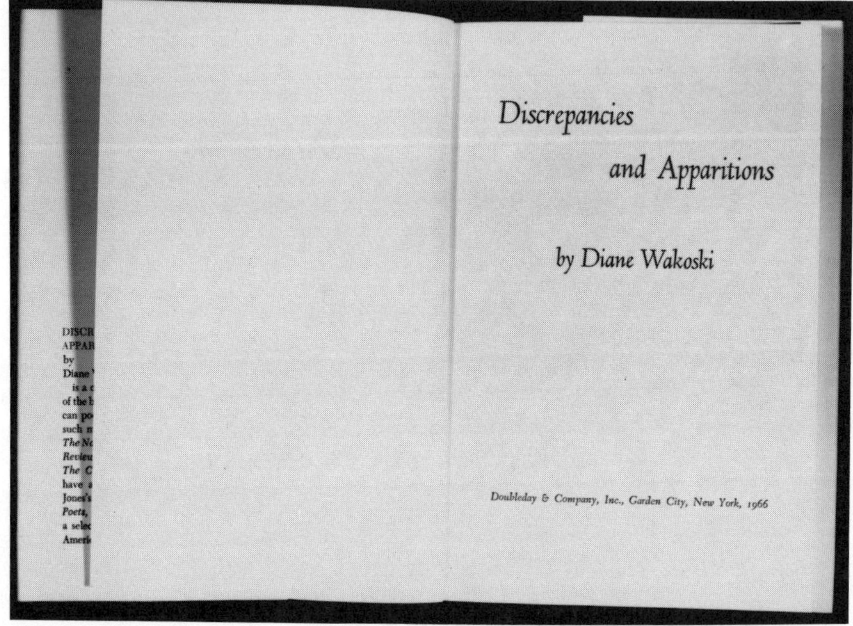

Title page of Discrepancies and Apparitions.

Paints Mountains," 68 "Death and the Miser," 70 "A Child, a Wasp, and an Apricot Tree," 72 "The Priestess No. 1," 74 "A Poem for the Yam Festival," 75 "Wind Secrets," 77 "Beyond All Sense of Time," 78 "Ordinary Poem," 82 "Tendencies We Have Already Seen," 86 "The Helms Bakery Man," 88 "The Piano," 89 "Possession Poem."

A4   The George Washington Poems   1967

(See photo page 9.)

[in black:] THE / GEORGE WASHINGTON / POEMS / Diane Wakoski / riverrun press / P.O. Box 557, Cooper Station / New York, N.Y. 10003

Collation: pp. [1–10] 11 [12] 13 [14] 15 [16] 17 [18] 19 [20] 21 [22] 23 [24] 25 [26] 27 [28] 29 [30] 31 [32] 33 [34] 35 [36] 37 [38] 39 [40] 41 [42] 43 [44] 45 [46] 47 [48] 49 [50] 51 [52] 53 [54] 55 [56]; 10 5/8″ × 8 3/8″; printed on wove paper.

Pagination: p. [1] price (see note below), p. [2] blank, p. [3] half-title, p. [4] dedication: "To My Father & My Husband," p. [5] title page, p. [6]

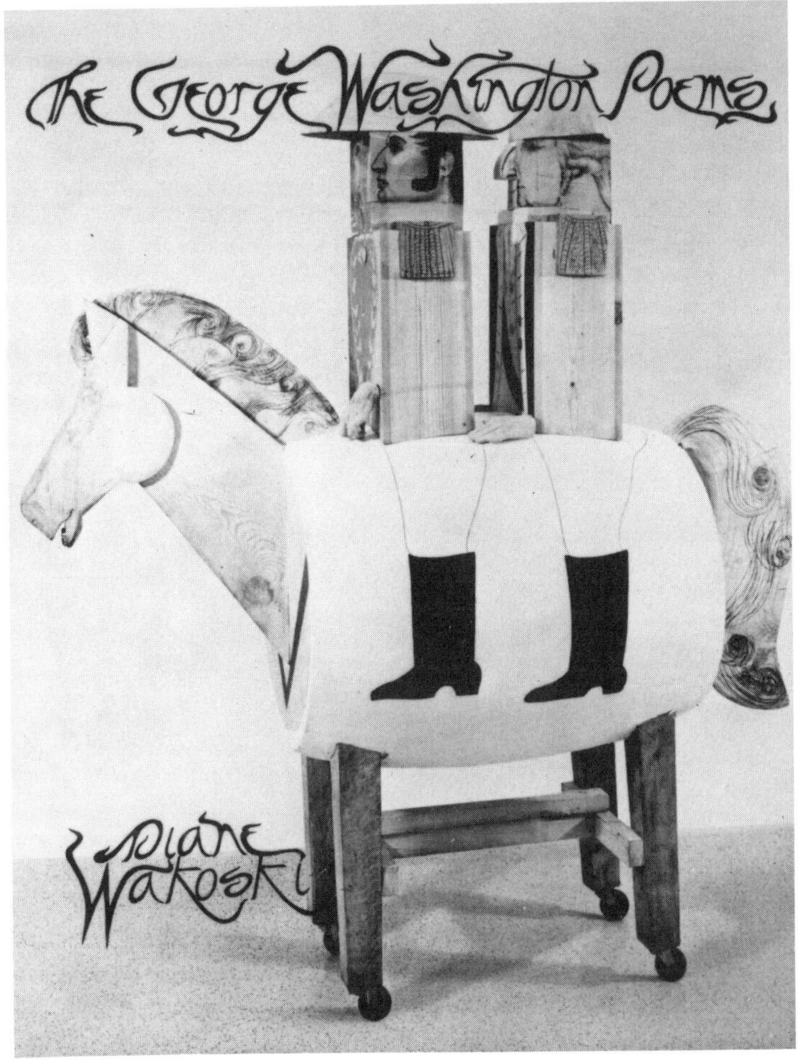

Dust jacket of The George Washington Poems.

copyright and acknowledgments, p. [7] contents, p. [8] blank, p. [9] half-title, p. [10] blank, pp. 11–[56] text.

Binding: Bound in green paper wrappers. Front cover: [reproducing calligraphic lettering, in black:] The George Washington Poems / Diane / Wakoski. Cover photograph, "The Generals," by Marisol.

Publication: Published by the Riverrun Press, New York, in 1967 at $2.00.

Contents: 11 "George Washington and the Loss of His Teeth," 13 "George Washington and the Dream of Gladys Hindmarch," 16 "George Washington Slept Here," 19 "George Washington," 21 "Waiting Under George Washington's Bridge," 23 "Exposition Is the Hard Part—the Rest Follows," 25 "George Washington and the Pearl Necklace," 27 "George Washington Meets Baudelaire," 28 "George Washington and the Invention of Dynamite," 29 "Patriotic Poem," 31 "Crossing the Delaware," 32 "Money over the Water," 34 "The Father of My Country," 38 "George Washington Absent from His Country," 40 "George Washington Hands the Keys to Uncle Sam," 42 "Uncle Sam in the White House," 43 "Between All Our Helloes & Goodbyes," 44 "George Washington, the Surveyor," 45 "Black Uncle Sam and Poor Ofay Me," 46 "Uncle Sam & the Good American Lady," 48 "George Washington Writes Home About Harvesting His Hemp," 50 "George Washington Dreams of Paratroop Forces," 52 "George Washington; the Whole Man."

Note: The price is given as follows, on p. [1], in black: Price: / [stamped and tilted:] 2 [reproduction of one-dollar bill]. In advance of publication, approximately 20 copies escaped the stamped number two.

A5   **The Diamond Merchant**   1968

[in red:] The Diamond Merchant / Diane Wakoski / [in black:] THE SANS SOUCI PRESS / *Cambridge, Massachusetts*

Collation: pp. [i–vi] [1–2] 3–16 [17–20] 21–34 [35–42]; 7 1/4″ × 5 1/2″; printed on wove paper.

Pagination: pp. [i–ii] blank, p. [iii] half-title, p. [iv] blank, p. [v] title page, p. [vi] copyright, p. [1] half-title, p. [2] blank, pp. 3–[17] text, p. [18] blank, p. [19] "Glass," p. [20] blank, pp. 21–[35] text, pp. [36–37] blank, p. [38] colophon: "This first edition of The Diamond Merchant is limited to 99 copies on Fabriano Book paper and one special large-paper copy on Shizuoka Vellum with the author's typescript bound in. Printed for William Young at the Sans Souci Press, June, 1968," pp. [39–42] blank.

Binding: Green cloth over boards. White paper label pasted on spine, reading downward: [in black:] Diane Wakoski / THE DIAMOND MERCHANT. Blue endpapers.

Dust jacket: Issued in a dark red paper dust jacket. White paper label pasted on front: [in black:] THE DIAMOND MERCHANT / Diane Wakoski.

Publication: Published by the Sans Souci Press, Cambridge, Massachusetts, in 1968.

Contents: 1 "The Diamond Merchant," 19 "Glass."

A6   Greed, Parts One and Two   1968

(a) *First edition*:

[in black:] GREED / parts one and two / Diane Wakoski / black sparrow press [centered dot] los angeles [centered dot] 1968

Collation: pp. [1–6] 7–11 [12–14] 15–23 [24]; 9 1/2″ × 6 3/8″; printed on wove paper.

Pagination: pp. [1–2] blank, p. [3] title page, p. [4] copyright, p. [5] "I. Of Polygamy," p. [6] blank, pp. 7–11 text, p. [12] blank, p. [13] "2. Of Accord & Principle," p. [14] blank, pp. 15–23 text, p. [24] colophon: "Designed and printed February, 1968 in Santa Barbara by / Alan Brilliant and Noel Young for the Black Sparrow Press. / Cover design by Barbara Martin. This edition is limited to / three hundred copies; fifty copies numbered 1–50 bound in / boards and two hundred and fifty copies numbered 51–300 / sewn in paper wrappers, all copies signed by the author."

Binding: Issued in light brown wrappers. Front, with design by Barbara Martin and linoleum cut by Alan Brilliant: [in red:] GREED / [in black:] parts one and two / [publisher's emblem] / Diane Wakoski. Sewn with brown thread.

Publication: Published by the Black Sparrow Press, Los Angeles, California, 5 April 1968, at $6.00. Edition size was 280 copies. 265 copies were signed by the author. 15 copies were numbered and marked "For Review."

Contents: "Greed, Parts One and Two."

(b) *Limited edition*:   1968

Title page, Collation, & Pagination as A6 a.

Binding: Issued in mustard paper over boards. Cover: as wrappered issue. White paper label pasted on spine, reading downward: [in black:] Diane Wakoski [dot] Greed. Tan flyleaves and endpapers.

Dust jacket: Issued in an unprinted white paper dust jacket.

Publication: Published by the Black Sparrow Press, Los Angeles, California, 5 April 1968, at $10.00. Edition size was 54 signed copies, of which two were marked "Printer's Copy" and one each as "Author's Copy" and "Publisher's Copy."

A7   Inside the Blood Factory   1968

(a) *First edition*:

[in black:] Inside / the Blood Factory / Diane Wakoski / 1968 / Doubleday & Company, Inc., Garden City, New York

Collation: pp. [1–8] 9–30 [31–32] 33–59 [60–62] 63–78 [79–80] 81–96; 5 3/8″ × 8 1/4″; printed on wove paper.

Pagination: p. [1] half-title, p. [2] books by DW, p. [3] title page, p. [4] copyright, pp. [5–6] contents, p. [7] "I / Blue Monday," p. [8] blank, pp. 9–30 text, p. [31] "II / Poems to The Man / in the Silver Ferrari," p. [32] blank, pp. 33–59 text, p. [60] blank, p. [61] "III / From The Tarot Deck," p. [62] blank, pp. 63–78 text, p. [79] "IV / The Ice Eagle," p. [80] blank, pp. 81–96 text.

Binding: Black cloth over boards. Stamped on spine, reading downward: [in silver:] Diane Wakoski [in red:] Inside the Blood Factory [in silver:] Doubleday. Red endpapers.

Dust jacket: Issued in white paper dust jacket. Front cover and spine: photograph by Alex Gotfryd. Front: [in black:] Inside / the Blood Factory / new poems / by Diane Wakoski. Spine, reading downward: [in black:] Inside the Blood Factory / Diane Wakoski / Doubleday. Back cover: blurb by Louis Simpson and selections from reviews of *Discrepancies and Apparitions*. Front flap: publisher's note on DW. Back flap: photograph of DW by Laurence Hellenberg and a biographical note.

Publication: Published by Doubleday & Company, New York, in 1968 at $4.50.

Contents: 9 "Blue Monday," 12 "The Night a Sailor Came to Me in a Dream," 13 "Sestina from the Home Gardener," 15 "Rain Trip," 16 "The Father of My Country," 21 "The House of the Heart," 23 "Water Shapes," 25 "Sleep Incantation," 27 "In Gratitude to Beethoven," 33 "This King: The Tombed Egyptian One," 34 "To the Man in the Silver Ferrari," 42 "Rescue Poem," 45 "Cerise," 48 "This Beautiful Black Marriage," 51 "Filling the Boxes of Joseph

Cornell," 57 "A Room Away from You," 62 "The Empress," 65 "The Empress No. 5," 66 "The Hermit," 67 "Sun," 68 "King of Pentacles: This Figure Has No Special Description," 71 "3 of Swords," 74 "Six of Cups," 77 "Looking for the Sign on Fulham Road," 81 "The Canoer," 82 "Ringless," 85 "The Blackbird," 86 "An Apology," 88 "Slicing Oranges for Jeremiah," 92 "Summer," 93 "The Ice Eagle."

(b) *Variant binding*:   1968

Title page, Collation, Pagination, Binding, Dust jacket, Publication, & Contents as A7 a, save with white endpapers.

(c) *First paper edition*:   1968

Title page, Collation, Pagination, & Contents as A7 a, save with addition of note, p. 47: "INSIDE THE BLOOD FACTORY was published simultaneously in a hardcover edition by Doubleday & Company, Inc."

Binding: Issued in stiff paper covers identical to dust jacket of A7 a, save without flaps and with price printed in black, upper right corner of front cover: $1.95.

Publication: Published by Doubleday & Company, New York, in 1968 at $1.95.

A8   The Magellanic Clouds (Recording)   1968

Collation: Recording; 14″ × 6 7/8″ folded to 7″ × 6 7/8″; 33 1/3 rpm recording on cover, over photograph of DW and target design. Perforated for spindle. Also reprints text.

Publication: Published by the Letter Edged in Black Press, Inc., in 1968.

A9   Greed, Parts 3 and 4   1969

(See photos pages 14 and 15.)

(a) *First edition*:

[in blue:] diane wakoski / [in red:] GREED / [in blue:] parts 3 and 4 / los angeles / black sparrow press / 1969

Diane Wakoski

Book cover of Greed, Parts 3 and 4, *first edition.*

Title page of Greed, Parts 3 and 4, *first edition.*

Collation: pp. [1–8] 9–18 [19–20] 21–29 [30–36]; 9 1/2″ × 6 1/4″; printed on wove paper.

Pagination: pp. [1–4] blank, p. [5] title page, p. [6] copyright and publisher's note on DW publications, p. [7] "GREED / PART III," p. [8] blank, pp. 9–18 text, p. [19] "GREED / PART IV, " p. [20] blank, pp. 21–29 text, pp. [30–32] blank, p. [33] publisher's note, emblem, and copy number, pp. [34–36] blank.

Binding: Issued in green paper wrappers, stapled, with green flyleaves tucked under unprinted flaps. Front, on green abstract design: [in grey:] diane wakoski / [in red:] GREED / [in grey:] parts 3 and 4.

Publication: Published by the Black Sparrow Press, Los Angeles, California, 13 October 1969, at $2.00. Edition size was 256 copies.

Contents: "Greed, Parts 3 and 4."

(b) *Variant binding*:   1969

Title page, Collation, Pagination, & Binding as A9 a, except sewn instead of stapled. Red thread with tie inside.

Publication: Published by the Black Sparrow Press, Los Angeles, California, 13 October 1969, at $5.00. Edition size was 300 signed and numbered copies.

(c) *Limited edition*:   1969

Title page, Collation, & Pagination as A9 a, save with one sheet removed, and pp. [1–2] and [35–36] are green flyleaves.

Binding: Issued in green paper over boards. Front: as wrapped issue. Green paper label pasted on spine, reading downward: [in gold:] Greed, Parts III & IV [dot] Diane Wakoski.

Dust jacket: Issued in a clear acetate dust jacket.

Publication: Published by the Black Sparrow Press, Los Angeles, California, 13 October 1969, at $10.00. Edition size was 160 signed copies. 150 copies were numbered 1–150. Five copies were numbered and marked "Presentation Copy." One copy each was marked "Author's Copy," "Publisher's Copy," "Printer's Copy," "Binder's Copy," and "File Copy."

A10   The Lament of the Lady Bank Dick   1969

(See photos pages 17 and 18.)

[between vertical red rules, in black:] Diane Wakoski / THE LAMENT / OF THE LADY / BANK DICK / Sans Souci Press / Cambridge, Massachusetts

Collation: pp. [1–24]; 9 5/8″ × 6 1/2″; printed on wove paper.

Pagination: pp. [1–2] blank, p. [3] half-title, p. [4] blank, p. [5] title page, p. [6] copyright, p. [7] half-title, p. [8] blank, p. [9] dedication, p. [10] blank, pp. [11–19] text, p. [20] blank, p. [21] colophon: ". . .limited to ninety-nine numbered copies, all signed by the author," p. [22] "Printed by William Ferguson / Cambridge, Massachusetts," pp. [23–24] blank.

Diane
Wakoski

THE LAMENT
OF THE LADY
BANK DICK

Book cover of The Lament of the Lady Bank Dick.

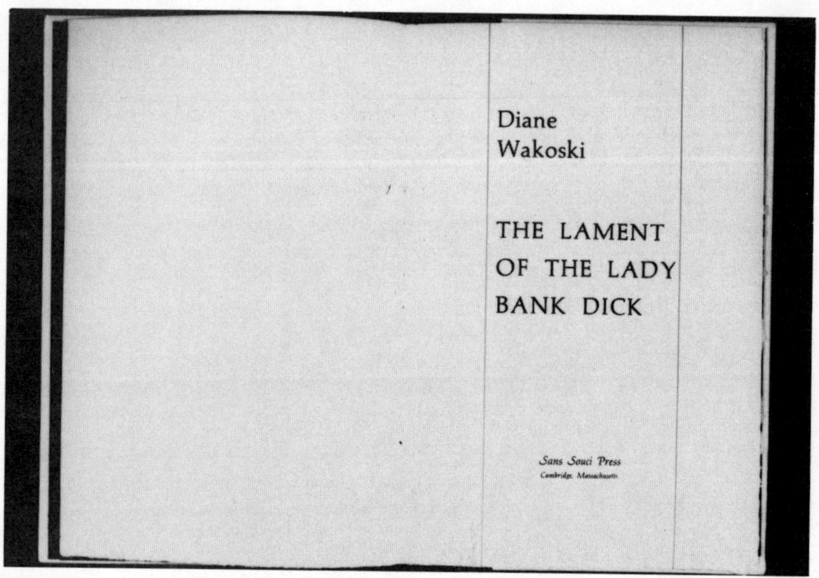

Title page of The Lament of the Lady Bank Dick.

Binding: Bound in half black cloth with white paper over boards. Front cover: [in black:] Diane / Wakoski / The LAMENT / OF THE LADY / BANK DICK. Black endpapers.

Dust jacket: Issued in a glassine dust jacket.

Publication: Published by the Sans Souci Press, Cambridge, Massachusetts, October 1969. Edition size was 109 copies. 99 copies were signed by the author and numbered 1–99. 10 copies were marked "For Presentation," signed by the author and the publisher (William Young), and numbered 1–10.

Contents: "The Lament of the Lady Bank Dick."

A11   Thanking My Mother for Piano Lessons   1969

[in black ornamental lettering:] THANKING MY / MOTHER FOR / PIANO LESSONS / DIANE WAKOSKI / [in black:] the perishable press limited postoffice box seven mount horeb wisconsin / all rights and copyright by diane wakoski nineteen hundred sixty nine

Collation: pp. [1–16]; 7 1/2″ × 5 3/8″; printed on wove paper.

Pagination: p. [1] half-title: [in orange:] TMMFPL [dot] DW, p. [2] blank, p. [3] title page, p. [4] blank, pp. [5–13] text, p. [14] blank, p. [15] colophon: "Two Hundred & fifty copies," and drawing, p. [16] blank.

Binding: Issued in brown laid paper wrappers. Sewn, with tie inside. Embossed on front cover: TMMFPL : DW.

Publication: Published by the Perishable Press, Mount Horeb, Wisconsin, in 1969. Edition size was 250 copies, of which 190 were for sale.

Contents: "Thanking My Mother for Piano Lessons."

Note: "This paper was couched on the 'magic felt' which was gratis from a papermill here in Wisconsin. It was loaded with pigment from its last job, so each pressing produced a different color in the sheet, beginning with a hot pink & lighter to an orange & on to Ivory & finally off-white with light tangerine deckles!"—Walter Hamady, *Two Decades of Hamady & The Perishable Press Limited.*

A12   Black Dream Ditty   1970

(a) *First edition*:

[above the first 17 lines of text, in orange:] BLACK DREAM DITTY FOR / BILLY "THE KID" M SEEN / IN DR. GENEROSITY'S BAR / RECRUITING FOR HELL'S / ANGELS AND BLACK MAFIA

Collation: pp. [1–4]; 6 5/8″ × 5″; printed on wove paper.

Pagination: p. [1] title page and text, pp. [2–3] text, p. [4] colophon: "Designed by Barbara Martin & printed / by Noel Young. Published for the / friends of the Black Sparrow Press / in an edition of 426 copies, / 126 of which have been numbered / & signed by the author."

Binding: Issued in stiff black paper wrappers. Front cover: [lettered in green with wavy baselines and irregular letters:] BLACK DREAM DITTY / FOR BILLY "THE KID" M / SEEN IN DR. GENEROSITY'S / BAR RECRUITING / FOR HELL'S ANGELS / AND BLACK MAFIA / BY DIANE WAKOSKI. Yellow flyleaves. Stapled.

Publication: Published by the Black Sparrow Press, Los Angeles, California, 15 July 1970, for distribution gratis. Edition size was 303 copies.

Contents: "Black Dream Ditty."

(b) *Variant binding*:   1970

Title page, Collation, Pagination, & Binding as A12 a, save sewn instead of stapled.

Publication: Published by the Black Sparrow Press, Los Angeles, California, 15 July 1970, for distribution gratis. Edition size was 105 signed copies. 100 copies were numbered 1–100 and 5 copies were unnumbered.

(c) *Limited edition*:   1970

Title page, Collation, & Pagination as A12 a.

Binding: Bound in multicolored cloth with floral design over boards. Front: black paper label pasted on and printed as wrappered issues. Brown endpapers and yellow flyleaves.

Publication: Published by the Black Sparrow Press, Los Angeles, California, 15 July 1970, for distribution gratis. Edition size was 35 signed copies. 26 copies were lettered A–Z. 4 copies were numbered and marked "Presentation Copy." 5 copies were marked one each as "Author's Copy," "Publisher's Copy," "Printer's Copy," "Binder's Copy," and "File Copy."

A13   Exorcism   1970

Collation: Broadside; 17″ × 10 7/8″; printed on wove paper.

Publication: Published by My Dukes, Cambridge, Massachusetts, in 1970. Edition size unknown. Approximately 10 copies have the last line changed and then signed by the author.

Contents: "Exorcism."

**A14   A Few Suggestions for Concerned Actions
             by People Who Love Poetry**   1970

[in black:] A few suggestions for concerned actions by people who love poetry / by Diane Wakoski

Collation: Photocopy of typescript; 1 leaf; title above text; 8 1/2" × 11".

Publication: Privately published in New York in September 1970. Edition size unknown.

Contents: "A few suggestions for concerned actions by people who love poetry."

A15   Love, You Big Fat Snail   1970

Collation: Broadside; 15 1/4" × 11 1/4"; printed on wove paper.

Publication: Published by The Tenth Muse, San Francisco, in 1970. Edition size was 218 copies, of which 18 were numbered and signed by the author.

Contents: "Love, You Big Fat Snail."

A16   The Magellanic Clouds   1970

(*See photos pages 22 and 23.*)

(a) *First edition*:

[double spread with grey cloud illustration, and in black:] the / magellanic clouds / diane wakoski / black sparrow press los angeles 1970

Collation: pp. [1–10] 11–150 [151–158]; 9 3/8" × 6 1/8"; printed on wove paper.

Pagination: p. [1] works by DW [The last entry, "The Moon Has A Complicated Georgraphy," is corrected with a blue erratum slip laid in.], pp. [2–3] title pages, p. [4] copyright and acknowledgments, p. [5] "For the man who loves me the most," p. [6] blank, pp. [7–8] contents, p. [9] reprints dictionary entry: Magellanic Clouds, p. [10] blank, pp. 11–150 text, pp. [151–152] blank, p. [153] colophon: "Printed January 1970 in Santa Barbara / by Noel Young for the Black Sparrow Press. / Design by Barbara Martin. This edition is / limited to 1000 copies in paper wrappers, / & 250 copies handbound in boards by / Earle Gray numbered & signed by the poet," p. [154] blank, p. [155] photograph of DW and poem: "The poet is the passionate man...," pp. [156–158] blank.

Binding: Bound in bluish grey wrappers with cloud design front and back. Front: [in black:] THE MAGELLANIC / CLOUDS / DIANE WAKOSKI.

     Diane Wakoski

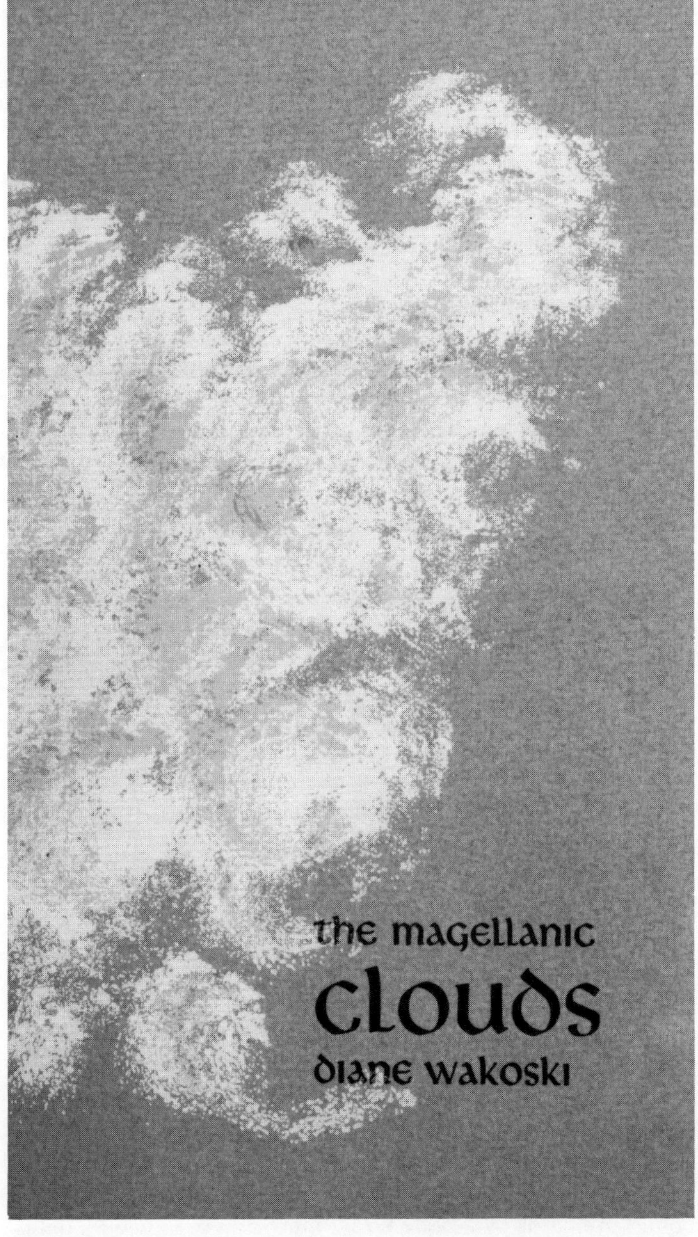

Book cover of The Magellanic Clouds, *first edition.*

Title page of The Magellanic Clouds, *first edition.*

Spine, reading downward: [in black:] DIANE WAKOSKI - THE MAGELLANIC CLOUDS - BLACK SPARROW PRESS. Blue flyleaves.

Publication: Published by the Black Sparrow Press, Los Angeles, California, 25 February 1970, at $4.00. Edition size was 1017 copies.

Contents: 11 "Greed: Part 1. Of Polygamy," 17 "Greed: Part 2. Of Accord & Principle," 27 "In Place of a Phone Call to Arabia," 28 "Reaching Out With the Hands of the Sun," 32 "The Queen of Night Walks Her Thin Dog," 34 "The Prince of Darkness Passing Through This House," 36 "The Cufflink Jade," 38 "The Day of the Autobiographical Frog," 44 "From the Eleventh Finger," 46 "The Singer," 47 "Poems From the Impossible," 50 "Adam," 51 "On the Prairie," 52 "Cast a Cold One," 53 "At Welsh's Tomb," 55 "Call Me Ishmael," 56 "The Buddha Inherits 6 Cars on His Birthday," 58 "Cinema II," 59 "The Eyes of Death Watering on the Desert," 62 "The Magician," 63 "Night Dangers," 65 "Love to My Electric Hand Mixer," 66 "My Face in the Palm of Your Hand," 68 "The Conjurer," 69 "Speonk Because It's a Favorite Word," 70 "The Acts of Devotion," 72 "The Gentleman's Terrified Stand-still," 73 "Now Perseus' Face," 77 "To the MGM Lion," 80 "The Universes," 86 "Lady's Poem," 87 "The Birds of Paradise Being Very Plain Birds,"

92 "Love Passes Beyond the Incredible Hawk of Innocence," 98 "The Old Impossibilities," 101 "I Can Taste Time on My Tongue Like Salt," 103 "The Dream Code," 106 "There's Plenty of Anguish at the Railroad," 108 "Thank You for the Valentine," 110 "The Magellanic Clouds," 113 "Everything Boils Down to Diamonds," 114 "My My They Cry," 115 "My Heart Has the Radio On All the Time," 118 "The Silver Psycho-Out," 120 "Diamond Story," 123 "Sometimes Even My Knees Smile," 124 "A Poet Recognizing the Echo of the Voice," 129 "Sister Diane's Book of the Zodiac," 138 "Exorcism," 140 "Finding a Husband in the Chinese Year of the Cock," 144 "A Poem for My 32nd Birthday."

Note: An unknown number of copies were issued prior to the addition of the erratum slip.

(b) *Variant binding*:   1970

Title page, Collation, Pagination & Contents as A16 a.

Binding: Bound in half blue cloth with light blue paper over boards. Front and back as wrappered issue. Grey paper label pasted on spine, reading downward: [in black:] DIANE WAKOSKI - THE MAGELLANIC CLOUDS. Blue endpapers.

Dust jacket: Issued in a clear acetate dust jacket.

Publication: Published by the Black Sparrow Press, Los Angeles, California, 25 February 1970, at $15.00. Edition size was 255 copies. 250 copies were numbered 1–250. One copy each was marked "Author's Copy," "Publisher's Copy," "Printer's Copy," "Binder's Copy," and "File Copy." The Author's and Publisher's copies were bound in half blue calf.

Note: The erratum slip was laid into all hardcover copies. The poem which appears beneath the photograph of DW on p. [155] is an edited version of "Poet at the Carpenter's Bench" (cf. A27).

**A17   Some Books Recommended by Diane Wakoski —
             Pertaining to Poetry**   1970

Collation: Mimeographed; 1 leaf; 8 1/2″ × 11″; title above text.

Publication: Privately published in New York in September 1970, edition size unknown.

Contents: "Some Books Recommended by Diane Wakoski—Pertaining to Poetry."

A18   Greed, Parts 5-7   1971

(a) *First edition*:

[in black:] DIANE WAKOSKI / GREED / PARTS 5-7 / [red sun device] / BLACK SPARROW PRESS LOS ANGELES 1971

Collation: pp. [1-6] 7-19 [20-22] 23-34 [35-36] 37-46 [47-52]; 9″ × 6″; printed on wove paper.

Pagination: pp. [1-2] blank, p. [3] title page, p. [4] copyright, p. [5] "GREED, PART 5 / The Shark—Parents & Children," p. [6] blank, pp. 7-19 text, p. [20] blank, p. [21] "GREED, PART 6 / Jealousy—A Confessional," p. [22] blank, pp. 23-34 text, p. [35] "GREED, PART 7 / Self-Righteousness," p. [36] blank, pp. 37-46 text, pp. [47-48] blank, p. [49] colophon: "Printed January 1971 in Santa Barbara / for the Black Sparrow Press by Noel Young. / Design by Barbara Martin. This edition is / limited to 1000 copies in paper wrappers; / 200 hardover copies numbered & signed / by the poet; & 26 lettered presentation copies / handbound in boards by Earle Gray, / signed & with an original holograph / poem by the poet," p. [50] blank, p. [51] photograph of DW and note on author, p. [52] blank.

Binding: Issued in pink paper wrappers. Front: [in black:] PARTS 5-7 / GREED / DIANE WAKOSKI. Spine, reading downward: [in dark brown:] GREED, Parts 5-7 [dot] DIANE WAKOSKI Black Sparrow Press. Orange flyleaves.

Publication: Published by the Black Sparrow Press, Los Angeles, California, 15 February 1971, at $3.00. Edition size was 1011 copies.

Contents: "Greed, Parts 5-7."

(b) *Hardcover edition*:   1971

Title page, Collation & Pagination as A18 a.

Binding: Bound in half striped, multicolored cloth with pink paper over boards. Front cover: as wrapped issue. Pink paper label pasted on spine, reading downward: [in black:] GREED, Parts 5-7 [dot] DIANE WAKOSKI. Orange endpapers.

26   Diane Wakoski

Publication: Published by the Black Sparrow Press, Los Angeles, California,
15 February 1971, at $15.00. Edition size was 201 signed copies. 200 copies
were numbered 1–200. One copy was marked "File Copy."

(c) *Limited edition*:   1971

Title page, Collation, Pagination, & *Binding* as A18 b, save bound in half red
cloth, instead of half striped cloth, and with extra leaf bound in before p. [1]
for holograph poem by DW.

Publication: Published by the Black Sparrow Press, Los Angeles, California,
15 February 1971, at $25.00. Edition size was 34 signed copies, each with a
holograph poem by the author bound in. 26 copies were lettered A-Z. One
copy each was marked "Author's Copy," "Publisher's Copy," "Printer's
Copy," "Binder's Copy," and "File Copy." Three copies were numbered and
marked "Presentation Copy."

Note: An examined copy had the holograph poem "A Shot or Two for Buffalo
Bill with Flourishes to Tony Weinberger" bound in. A flyer, 8″ × 3 1/2″ on
pink paper, preceded publication.

A19   The Motorcycle Betrayal Poems   1971

(*See photos pages 27 and 28.*)

(a) *First edition*:

[rule of eight black dots] / [in black:] THE MOTORCYCLE BETRAYAL
POEMS / [rule of eight black dots] / SIMON AND SCHUSTER [dot]
NEW YORK

Collation: pp. [1–6] 7–8 [9–10] 11–41 [42] 43–83 [84–86] 87–160; 8 1/4″ × 5 1/2″;
printed on wove paper.

Pagination: [1] publisher's emblem, p. [2] books by DW, p. [3] title page, p.
[4] copyright, p. [5] dedication: "This book is dedicated to all those men /
who betrayed me at one time or another, / in hopes they will fall off their
motorcycles / and break their necks," p. [6] blank, pp. 7–8 contents, p. [9]
half-title, p. [10] blank, pp. 11–41 text, p. [42] blank, pp. 43–83 text, p. [84]
blank, p. [85] "FIVE LOVE POEMS," p. [86] blank, pp. 87–160 text.

Binding: Bound in marbleized grey and white paper over boards. Spine,
reading downward: [in red:] [6 dots] THE MOTORCYCLE BETRAYAL
POEMS [6 dots] [slash] DIANE WAKOSKI [10 dots] SIMON AND
SCHUSTER. White endpapers.

Dust jacket of The Motorcyle Betrayal Poems, *first edition.*

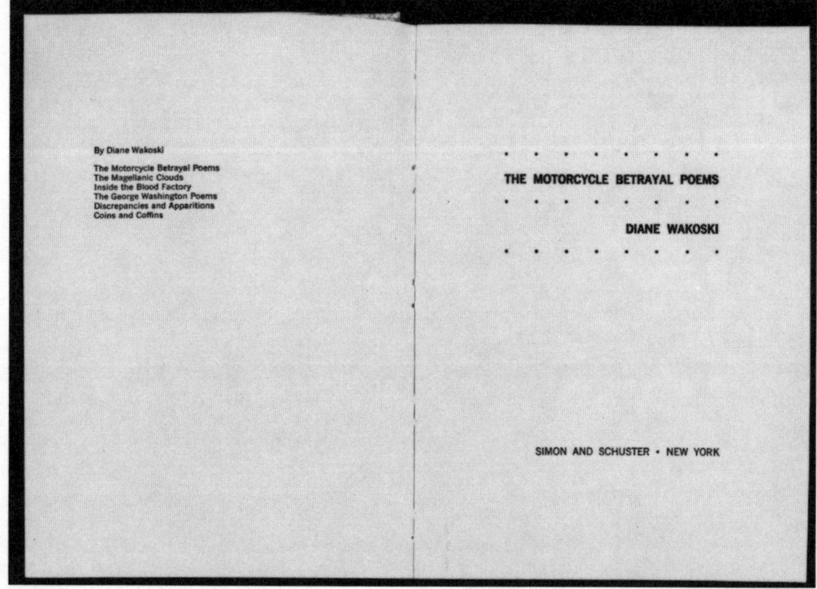

Title page for The Motorcycle Betrayal Poems, *first edition.*

Dust jacket: Issued in a black paper dust jacket. Front: [photograph, in negative, of motorcycle and, in white:] THE / MOTORCYCLE / BETRAYAL / POEMS / BY / DIANE / WAKOSKI. Back cover: [photograph of DW by Tom Victor and, overlaid in white:] "The Most vital and / accomplished of / young American poets / - Book Week. Spine, reading downward: [in white:] THE MOTORCYCLE BETRAYAL POEMS BY DIANE WAKOSKI SIMON AND SCHUSTER. Front flap: [in black:] To read this book / is to meet / an extraordinary woman. / $5.95. Back flap: publisher's note on DW.

Publication: Published by Simon and Schuster, New York, in 1971 at $5.95.

Contents: 11 "I Have Had to Learn to Live With My Face," 16 "Love Letter Postmarked Van Beethoven," 19 "Uneasy Rider," 21 "Bloodroot," 23 "The Desert Motorcyclist," 24 "My Hell's Angel," 31 "Thanking My Mother for Piano Lessons," 36 "What I Want in a Husband Besides a Mustache," 40 "Indian Giver," 41 "Anticipation of Sharks," 43 "Letters to Shep," 49 "The Moon Being the Number 19," 53 "The Moon Has a Complicated Geography," 58 "For a (1) Cold, (2) Hard, (3) Mean, (4) Nasty, (5) None of These Sculptor I Like," 62 "I Lay Next to You All Night, Trying Awake to Understand the Watering Places of the Moon," 66 "No More Soft Talk," 69 "The Equinox," 72 "Film: Called 5 Blind Men," 75 "Love Song to Julian Harmony,"

76 "Love Song for David Garrison," 77 "Love Song for Gordon Quails," 78 "Love Song to Carl Scandor," 79 "Love Song for O.K. Ready," 82 "To the Champ of Pinball Machine Baseball," 87 "Five Love Poems," 88 "Sun Flowers in My Wrist," 90 "The Catalogue of Charms," 93 "The Lament of the Lady Bank Dick," 98 "The Ten-Dollar Cab Ride," 103 "With Words," 106 "Citizen's Trust," "Poem to a Man With Good Taste," 107 "Black Leather Because Bumblebees Look Like It," 108 "To Celebrate My Body," 111 "The Mechanic," 113 "To the Wives," 116 "Caves," 119 "Ten, the Number of My Fingers," 130 "Conversations with Jan," 142 "Reminding Me of Your Own Dead Sea of Silence," 143 "You, Letting the Trees Stand As My Betrayer," 145 "Music," "My Marriage Certificate," 146 "Glass," 153 "Fire Island Poem," 156 "Quicksilver Sailor's Daughter," 157 "The Pink Dress."

Notes: An examined copy had a publisher's card laid in: "Did you like this book?" Some copies, number unknown, are marked "First printing." Uncorrected proofs in printed wrappers preceded publication. A flyer issued in advance of publication contained blurbs by Denise Levertov, James Wright, Joyce Carol Oates, and Richard Eberhart.

(b) *First paper edition*:   1971

Title page, Collation, Pagination, & Contents as A19 a, save measures 8 1/4" × 5 3/8".

Binding: Issued in a stiff black paper wrapper. Front cover: [in green:] \$1.95 / [in white:] This book is dedicated to / all those men who betrayed / me at one time or another, / in hopes they will fall off / their motocycles and / break their necks. / THE MOTOCYCLE BETRAYAL POEMS / BY DIANE WAKOSKI /. Cover photograph by Tom Victor. Back cover: quotations from reviews of hardcover edition. Inside front and back covers: list of Touchstone Clarion Books. Spine, reading downward: [in white:] THE MOTORCYCLE BETRAYAL POEMS WAKOSKI [in green:] Simon and Schuster [publisher's emblem in white].

Publication: Published by Simon and Schuster/Touchstone in 1971 at \$1.95.

A20   On Barbara's Shore   1971

(a) *First edition*:

[within yellow rule frame, in black:] ON BARBARA'S / SHORE [in green:] A POEM BY / DIANE WAKOSKI / [in black:] BLACK SPARROW PRESS / LOS ANGELES 1971

Collation: pp. [1–12]; 8" × 4 5/8"; printed on wove paper.

Pagination: pp. [1-2] blank, p. [3] title page, p. [4] copyright, p. [5] dedication ("for Barbara"), p. [6] blank, pp. [7–9] text, p. [10] blank, p. [11] colophon: "On Barbara's Shore is the one hundredth / publication of the Black Sparrow Press. / It has been published gratis in / January 1971 both in wrappers & in a / hardcover edition limited to one / hundred numbered copies signed by / the author," p. [12] blank.

Binding: Issued in blue paper wrappers. Front: [within white rule frame, in black:] ON / BARBARA'S / SHORE / [reproduction of drawing in white of bird and leaves] / DIANE WAKOSKI. Sewn with tie inside. Brown flyleaves.

Publication: Published by the Black Sparrow Press, Los Angeles, California, on 10 February 1971. Edition size was 404 copies.

Contents: "On Barbara's Shore."

(b) *Limited edition*:   1971

Title page, Collation, & Pagination as A20 a, save measures 8 1/4" × 4 7/8".

Binding: Issued in half multicolored, patterned cloth with blue paper boards. Cover is printed as wrappered issue. Brown endsheets.

Publication: Published by the Black Sparrow Press, Los Angeles, California, on 10 February 1971. Edition size was 109 copies, of which 100 were numbered 1–100, 4 were marked as Publisher, Printer, Binder, and File copies, and 5 were numbered and marked "Author's Copy."

A21   **This Water Baby**   1971

Collation: Postcard; 6 1/2" × 5"; printed on lavender wove paper.

Publication: Published by the Unicorn Press, Santa Barbara, California, in 1971. The size of the trade edition is unknown. 50 copies were signed by the author and issued in a plastic cover entitled *Signed Edition of Fifty Copies*.

Contents: "This Water Baby."

Note: An unknown number of copies were gathered with seven other postcards and issued in 1972 as the *Unicorn Postcard Series II* (B5).

A22 The Water Element Song for Sylvia 1971

[typed, at top of first page:] The Water Element Song for Sylvia / for Sylvia Plath, a beautiful poet, / and my friends, Kathy Salonstall, / J + J + Wilson and the Martins

Collation: pp. [1–5]; 8 1/2″ × 14″; photocopied.

Pagination: p. [1] title and text, pp. [2–4] text, p. [5] text and date.

Contents: "The Water Element Song for Sylvia."

Publication: Typed and photocopied by DW and sent to a few of her friends, 9 July 1971, edition size unknown.

A23 Claws 1972

Collation: Postcard; 4″ × 5 7/8″; printed on dark red wove paper.

Publication: Published by the Burning Deck Press, Providence, Rhode Island, in 1972. Size of the edition is unknown.

Contents: "Claws."

Note: 100 copies were gathered in *Burning Deck Postcards: The Second Ten* (B7). An unknown number of copies were gathered in *Diane Wakoski / 2 broadsides, 3 postcards* (A41).

A24 A Lover Disregards Names 1972

Collation: Postcard; 5 7/8″ × 7″; printed on orange wove paper.

Publication: Published by the Burning Deck Press, Providence, Rhode Island, in 1972. The size of the edition is unknown.

Contents: "A Lover Disregards Names."

Note: An unknown number of copies were gathered in *Diane Wakoski / 2 broadsides, 3 postcards* (A41).

A25   The Pumpkin Pie   1972

(a) *First edition*:

[in orange:] The / PUMPKIN / Pie, or / Reassurances Are / Always False,
tho / We Love Them. Only / Physics Counts [3 orange dots] / [in grey:]
DIANE WAKOSKI

Collation: pp. [1–14]; 5 5/8″ × 4 1/2″; printed on wove paper.

Pagination: p. [1] A / Christmas / Greeting / from / the / Black / Sparrow /
Press / [publisher's emblem], p. [2] copyright, p. [3] half-title, p. [4] blank,
pp. 5–14] text. Colophon is printed on recto of back flyleaf: [publisher's
emblem] / Design by Barbara Martin. / Printed December 1972 for / the
Black Sparrow Press by / Noel Young. 126 copies / of this edition have / been
handbound in boards by / Earle Gray & are numbered / & signed by the
author.

Binding: Issued in stiff orange paper wrappers. Front: [in blue-green:] The
/ PUMPKIN / Pie. Sewn with tie inside. Issued in a white laid paper mailing
envelope, printed with publisher's emblem and address. Blue-green
flyleaves.

Publication: Published by the Black Sparrow Press, Los Angeles, California,
11 December 1972, for distribution gratis. Edition size was 431 copies.

Contents: "The Pumpkin Pie."

Note: An examined copy had a presentation card laid in: "COMPLIMENTS
/ of the / PUBLISHER / [publisher's emblem] / [publisher's address]. The
first eight copies printed had a misplaced line. The line "in any other room
of the house" appears on p. [14] in these copies, which were unsewn and
unissued.

(b) *Hardcover edition*:   1972

Title page, Collation, & Pagination as A25 a.

Binding: Bound in orange paper over boards and printed as wrappered issue.

Publication: Published by the Black Sparrow Press, Los Angeles, California,
11 December 1972, for distribution gratis. Edition size was 137 signed copies.
100 copies were numbered 1–100 and 26 copies were lettered. 5 copies were
numbered and marked "Author's Copy." One copy each was marked
"Publisher's Copy," "Printer's Copy," and "Binder's Copy." Three copies may
have been marked "File Copy."

A26   The Purple Finch Song   1972

Collation: Broadside; 14″ × 6 3/4″; printed on wove paper.

Publication: Published by the Perishable Press, Mt. Horeb, Wisconsin, in 1972. Edition size was 97 copies.

Contents: "The Purple Finch Song."

A27   Smudging   1972

(a) *First edition*:

[in orange:] SMUDGING / [in red:] by / Diane / Wakoski / [in black:] black sparrow press [dot] los angeles [dot] 1972

Collation: pp. [1–8] 9–68 [69–70] 71–106 [107–108] 109–153 [154–156]; 9″ × 6″; printed on wove paper.

Pagination: p. [1] blank, p. [2] works by DW, p. [3] title page, p. [4] copyright and acknowledgments, pp. [5–6] table of contents, p. [7] "I. DEFINI-TIONS," p. [8] blank, pp. 9–68 text, p. [69] "II. STATEMENTS," p [70] blank. pp. 71–106 text, p. [107] "III. PERSONALITIES," p. [108] blank, pp. 109–153 text, p. [154] blank, p. [155] colophon: "Printed May 1972 in Santa Barbara for the / Black Sparrow Press by Noel Young. Design by / Barbara Martin. This edition is published in / paper wrappers; there are 250 hard-cover copies / numbered & signed by the poet; & 30 / copies handbound in boards by Earle Gray / signed & with an original holograph poem by / the poet," p. [156] photograph of DW by Thomas Victor and publisher's note on DW.

Binding: Issued in light brown wrappers. Front: [in black:] SMUDGING [in blue:] : to smoke / or to protect against frost (as an / orchard) by means of smudge. / [in orange:] DIANE [in red:] WAKOSKI. Spine: [in black:] SMUDGING / Diane Wakoski / Black Sparrow Press. Black flyleaves.

Publication: Published by the Black Sparrow Press, Los Angeles, 15 May 1972 at $4.00 Edition size was 2510 copies.

Contents: 9 "Smudging," 14 "Greed, 3 & 4," 30 "Poet at the Carpenter's Bench," 33 "The Poem," 34 "The Mind, Like an Old Fish," 36 "Set: The Okapi," 37 "The Well Informed," 38 "When the Shoe Fits," 39 "My Trouble," 40 "Steely Silence," 41 "Children Visit the Island," 42 "To a Friend Who Can-not Accept My Judgement of Him," 45 "Ladies, Listen to Me," 47 "My

Knees Go Before the Firing Squad," 50 "Item 556-50-8853 From the
Perishing Person Catalogue," 52 "The Night Rides of My Neighbor Lorca,
That Prevent Sleep," 55 "The Empress # 8," 56 "# 18," 57 "To an Autocrat,"
60 "Settling the Issue," 61 "Fire," 62 "Without Desolation," 63 "Nobody Loves
Me, Not Even the Voles, Hyraxes, Or Elephants," 64 "Sour Milk," 66
"Smallness," 67 "Sun Poem," 68 "Poem Dressed in a White Baggy Suit," 71
"Anger at the Weather," 73 "Winter Ode," 74 "Overweight Poem," 76 "When
Metaphor Replaces Meteor Showers," 77 "To Bed," 78 "The Moon Explodes
in Autumn, As a Milkweed Pod," 81 "Water Under the Bridge," 83 "Her
Throat," 84 "To Open Use a Cornelian Key," 85 "The Duchess Potatoes,"
86 " Love Poem to the Magician," 87 "My Little Heart Pops Out, Like
Springs," 88 "Love Poem," 89 "With Rings on Her Fingers & Bells on Her
Toes, She Shall Have Music Wherever She Goes," 92 "Feet on the Ground,"
94 "Screw, a Technical Love Poem," 96 "My Legs," 99 "My Mother Tries
to Visit Me in the Dead of the Night," 100 "Placing a $2 Bet for a Man Who
Will Never Go to the Horse Races Anymore," 102 "Love Is Just an Old
Buick," 105 "A Winter Poem for Tony Weinburger Written on the Occasion
of Feeling Very Happy," 109 "Fanny's Cold Blue Eyes," 114 "The Pterodac-
tyl," 116 "A Poem to Celebrate Long Life," 117 "The Empress," 118 "Portrait
of a Lady," 120 "Vulture," 121 "Stories for Buflalo," 125 "Who Is My King of
Spain," 126 "The Imaginary Print of Your Spanish Foot," 127 "Poem for Judy
Garland, Which Is a Field Guide to Butterflies," 131 "Wishbones," 134 "The
Mariachis — A Glimpse," 137 "Handbook of Marriage & Wealth," 143 "The
Joyful Black Demon of Sister Clara Flies through the Midnight Woods on
Her Snowmobile," 151 "On Barbara's Shore."

(b) *Hardcover edition*:   1972

Title page, Collation, Pagination, & Contents as A27 a.

Binding: Bound in half orange cloth with light brown boards. Front: as A27 a.
Light brown paper label pasted on spine: [in black:] SMUDGING / Diane
Wakoski. Black endsheets. False headband.

Dust jacket: Issued in a clear acetate dust jacket.

Publication: Published by the Black Sparrow Press, Los Angeles, 15 May 1972
at $15.00. Edition size was 251 copies, with 250 signed by the author and
numbered, and one copy marked "File Copy."

(c) *Limited edition*:   1972

Title page, Collation, Pagination, Binding, & Contents as A27 b, save with extra
leaf bound in before first page for holograph poem by DW, and with half
multicolored instead of half orange cloth.

Publication: Published by the Black Sparrow Press, Los Angeles, 15 May 1972 at $30.00. Edition size was 39 signed coies. According to the publisher, "30 copies (numbered 1–30) were for sale, and 9 copies (1 each marked 'Author's Copy,' 'Publisher's Copy,' 'Binder's Copy,' and 'File Copy'; and 4 numbered and marked 'Presentation Copy') not for sale."

Note: An examined copy had the holograph poem "Would That Men Shake Their Trees" bound in. An advertising flyer designated "Broadside/Flyer No. 1," printing one poem from the book, preceded publication. 100 copies were signed by the author and numbered.

A28   Sometimes a Poet Will Hijack the Moon   1972

(*See photo page 36.*)

Collation: Broadside; 10″ × 11″; printed on wove paper.

Publication: Published by the Burning Deck Press, Providence, Rhode Island, in 1972. Size of the trade edition is unknown. Approximately 20 copies were signed by the author.

Contents: "Sometimes a Poet Will Hijack the Moon."

Note: Some copies were gathered in *Diane Wakoski / 2 broadsides, 3 postcards* (A41).

A29   Comparisons   1973

Collation: Postcard; 4 5/8″ × 7″; printed on white wove paper.

Publication: Published by the Burning Deck Press, Providence, Rhode Island, in 1973. Size of the edition is unknown.

Contents: "Comparisons."

Note: 150 copies were gathered in *Burning Deck Postcards: The Third Ten* (B8). An unknown number of copies were gathered in *Diane Wakoski / 2 broadsides, 3 postcards* (A41).

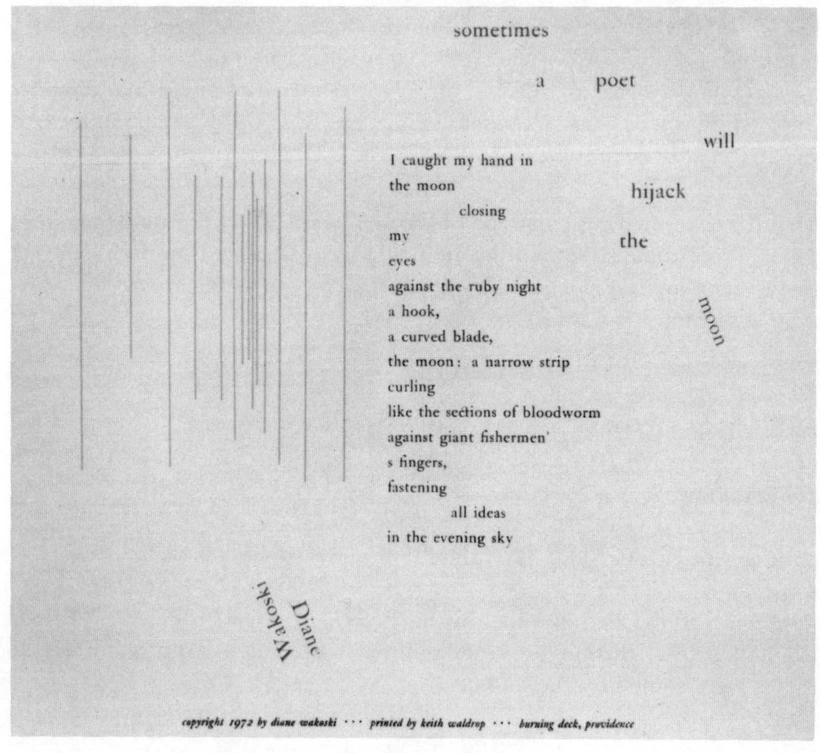

Broadside: Sometimes a Poet Will Hijack the Moon.

A30   Dancing on the Grave of a Son of a Bitch   1973

(a) *First edition*:

[in dull violet:] DIANE WAKOSKI / [green rule] / [in dull violet: DANC-
ING ON THE / GRAVE OF A SON / OF A BITCH [three green flower
ornaments] / [in dull violet:] Black Sparrow Press - Los Angeles - 1973

Collation: pp. [1-12] 13-54 [55] 56-73 [74-76] 77-109 [110-112] 113-121
[122-124] 125-137 [138-142]; 9″ × 6″; printed on wove paper.

Pagination: p. [1] blank, p. [2] works by DW, p. [3] title page, p. [4]
copyright, p. [5] blank, pp. [6-8] contents, p. [9] dedication: "for the King
of Spain whose footprints / I find wherever I go-," p. [10] blank, p. [11] "THE
ASTRONOMER POEMS," p. [12] blank, pp. 13-54 text, p. [55] "DANC-
ING ON THE GRAVE / OF A SON OF A BITCH," pp. 56-73 text, p.
[74] blank, p. [75] "SOME POEMS FOR THE BUDDHA'S BIRTHDAY,"

p. [76] blank, pp. 77–109 text, p. [110] blank, p. [111] "THE DIAMOND MERCHANT," p. [112] blank, pp. 113–121 text, p. [122] blank, p. [123] "ESOTERIC FABLES," p. [124] blank, pp. 125–137 text, p. [138] blank, p. [139] colophon: "Printed October 1973 in Santa Barbara for the Black / Sparrow Press by Noel Young. Design by Barbara / Martin. This edition is published in paper wrappers; / there are 300 hardcover copies numbered & signed by / the poet; & 50 copies handbound in boards by Earle / Gray signed & with an original holograph poem by the poet," p. 140 blank, p. 141 photograph of DW by Thomas Victor and publisher's note: "Diane Wakoski was born in California in 1937. / The poems in her published books give all the / important information about her life," p. [142] blank.

Binding: Issued in tan paper covers. Front: [in dull violet:] Dancing / on the / Grave / of / a / Son Of a Bitch / [rule of orange flower ornaments] / [in dull violet:] by / Diane / Wakoski. Spine, reading downward: [in dull violet:] DANCING ON THE GRAVE OF A SON OF A BITCH / : / DIANE WAKOSKI / Black Sparrow Press. Orange flyleaves.

Publication: Published by the Black Sparrow Press, Los Angeles, California, 23 November 1973, at $4.00. Edition size was 2530 coies.

Contents: 13 "Some Brilliant Sky," 15 "In This Galaxy," 16 "A Feather in Your Cap," 18 "The Moon Is Only Aggressive When You Are There," 19 "The Stargazer," 20 "An Ode to My Favorite Astronomer," 21 "In the Secret Room, East of the Sun, West of the Moon," 23 "The Mirror of a Day Chiming Marigold," 25 "The Sun Has an Angry Face," 26 "Meeting an Astronomer on the Buddha's Birthday," 27 "I Take Green Greed onto the Freeway," 28 "Looking for Rabbit Tracks on the Freeway," 30 "Those Trigger Fish Again," 31 "Fighting My Way Upstream, a Gar, a Bluefish, In My Foot," 32 "When Black Is a Color Because It Follows a Grey Day," 33 "The Gold Fish in the Cool Night," 35 "The Cool Star," 36 "For Gary, When My Hands Are over the Sun," 38 "Sun Gods Have Sun Spots," 39 "What Color Is the Mustache of the Sun," 40 "When You Throw Amber into the Well of the Moon," 42 "Wolf Fire," 43 "I Am the Daughter of the Sun," 45 "Counting Shooting Stars in the Eyes of an Invisible Opponent," 46 "Trying to Read by the Light of Shooting Stars," 47 "Market Scene on a Half Moon Trip," 49 "The Dream of Angling, the Dream of Cool Rain," 50 "Exchanging a Zebra for Your Favorite Girl/Desert/Moon," 52 "A Tiger Walks the Streets of an Old Town," 54 "For Whitman," 57 "Dancing on the Grave of a Son of a Bitch," 60 "The Purple Finch Song," 62 "A Little Mantra for Becky's Box," 63 "Snow Chant," 65 "A Sunset Chant," 66 "A Chant for Hyacinths," 67 "A Chant for the Dweller in the Desert Solitaire," 68 "Snowman Chant," 69 "Chant for a Sharp Knife," 71 "Apple Chant, 1," 72 "Apple Chant, 2," 73 "Chants/Chance," 77 "Buddha's Birthday," 78 "A Long Trainride Without a

Calendar Showing Buddha's Birthday," 79 "Letter to Carol Bergé on Buddha's Birthday," 81 "Judge Not, Says the Buddha on His Birthday," 82 "The Buddha Learns to Work a Radial Arm Saw on His Birthday," 83 "George Washington Sends a Pair of Shoebuckles to the Buddha on His Birthday," 84 "A Little Poem for the Calligrapher on the Buddha's Birthday," 86 "My Aunt Ella Meets the Buddha on His Birthday," 90 "That Delicate Displacement of Reality on the Buddha's Birthday," 91 "Buddha Has His Birthday in Court," 92 "A Chain Letter for Luck on the Buddha's Birthday," 93 "Instruction for Growing Laburnum on the Buddha's Birthday," 94 "Poem for the Comfortable on the Buddha's Birthday," 95 "The Scissors, a Poem for the Buddha's Birthday," 96 "The Blue World Holds the Sun as a Rake on Buddha's Birthday," 98 "A Message to Someone I Love on Buddha's Birthday," 99 "Poem for a Man Who Is Sleeping on the Buddha's Birthday," 100 "The Buddha Runs a Race on His Birthday," 101 "The Buddha Turns Base Metals, Flowers & Butterflies into Gold on His Birthday," 102 "The Buddha Meets Saturn," 104 "Bank Statement on the Buddha's Birthday," 105 "The Buddha Tags a Fish on His Birthday," 106 "Wildflowers for the Buddha on His Birthday," 107 "Poem for a Little Boy on the Buddha's Birthday," 108 "The Buddha Empties a Volcano on His Birthday," 109 "The Elephant & the Butterfly Meet on the Buddha's Birthday," 113 "The Diamond Merchant," 119 "A Long Poem for Eleanor Who Collects the Blood of Poets," 125 "A Short Fable of Endurance and Pity," 128 "The Owl and the Snake," 129 "The Cat With the Broken Tail," 132 "The Frog Who Was Born With a Wart on His Nose," 134 "The Fable of the Fragile Butterfly."

(b) *Hardcover edition*: 1973

Title page, Collation, Pagination, & Contents as A30 a.

Binding: Bound in half orange cloth with tan paper over boards. Tan paper label pasted on spine, reading downward: [in grey:] DANCING ON THE GRAVE OF A SON OF A BITCH / : / DIANE WAKOSKI. Orange endpapers.

Dust jacket: Issued in a clear acetate dust jacket.

Publication: Published by the Black Sparrow Press, Los Angeles, California, 23 November 1973, at $15.00. Edition size was 301 signed copies. 300 copies were numbered 1–300. One copy was marked "File copy."

(c) *Limited edition*: 1973

Title page, Collation, Pagination, Binding, Dust jacket & Contents as A30 b, save bound in half multicolored cloth, instead of half orange cloth, and with an extra leaf bound in between pp. [4–5] for a holograph poem by the author.

Publication: Published by the Black Sparrow Press, Los Angeles, California, 23 November 1973, at $25.00. Edition size was 55 signed copies. 50 copies were numbered 1–50. One each of five copies was marked "Author's Copy," "Publisher's Copy," "Printer's Copy," "Binder's Copy," and "File Copy."

Note: An examined copy had the holograph poem "Luxury" bound in.

A31   Greed / Parts 8, 9, 11   1973

(a) *First edition*:

[in purple:] GREED [slash] PARTS 8, 9, 11 / [blue rule] / [in orange:] DIANE WAKOSKI / [in blue:] BLACK SPARROW PRESS [slash] LOS ANGELES [slash] 1973

Collation: pp. [1–8] 9–15 [16–18] 19–31 [32–34] 35–50 [51–56]; 9″ × 6 1/8″; printed on wove paper.

Pagination: pp. [1–2] blank, p. [3] title page, p. [4] copyright, p. [5] Contents, p. [6] blank, p. [7] "GREED [slash] PART 8," p. [8] blank, pp. 9–15 text, p. [16] blank, p. [17] "GREED [slash] PART 9," p. [18] blank, pp. 19–31 text, p. [32] blank, p. [33] "GREED [slash] PART 11," p. [34] blank, pp. 35–50 text, pp. [51–52] blank, p. [53] colophon: "Printed May 1973 in Santa Barbara for the / Black Sparrow Press by Noel Young. Design by / Barbara Martin. This edition is published / in paper wrappers; there are 250 hardcover / copies numbered & signed by the poet; / & 50 copies handbound in boards / by Earle Gray, signed & with an original / holograph poem by the poet," p. [54] blank, p. [55] T. Victor photograph of DW and publisher's note on the author, p. [56] blank.

Binding: Bound in light blue wrappers. Front: [in red:] GREED / [red rule] / [in blue:] PARTS 8, 9, 11 / [18 blue rules, 1 red rule, 3 blue rules]/ [in blue:] DIANE WAKOSKI. Spine, reading downward: [in blue:] Greed [slash] Parts 8, 9, 11 [blue dot] DIANE WAKOSKI BLACK SPARROW PRESS. Purple flyleaves.

Publication: Published by the Black Sparrow Press, Los Angeles, California, 14 May 1973, at $3.00. Edition size was 2497 copies.

Contents: Greed, Part 8, p. 9, is "The Desire To Be What One Is Not While Clinging To What One Is." Part 9, p. 19, is "The Water Element Song for Sylvia." Part 11, p. 35, is "Power."

(b) *Hardcover edition*:   1973

Title page, Collation, Pagination, & Contents as A31 a.

Binding: Bound in half blue cloth with light blue paper over boards. Front
cover: as wrappered issue. White paper label pasted on spine, reading
downward: [in blue:] GREED [slash] PARTS 8, 9, 11 [bluc dot] DIANE
WAKOSKI. Purple endpapers.

Dust jacket: Issued in a clear acetate dust jacket.

Publication: Published by the Black Sparrow Press, Los Angeles, California,
14 May 1973, at $15.00. Edition size was 251 signed copies. 250 copies were
numbered 1–250. One copy was marked "File Copy."

(c) *Limited edition*:   1973

Title page, Collation, Pagination, Binding, & Contents as A31 b, save bound in
half patterned, multicolored cloth, instead of blue cloth, and with extra leaf
bound in between pp. 4–5 for holograph poem by DW.

Publication: Published by the Black Sparrow Press, Los Angeles, California,
14 May 1973, at $25.00. Edition size was 60 signed copies, each with a
holograph poem by the author bound in. 50 copies were numbered 1–50.
Five copies were numbered and marked "Presentation Copy." One copy each
was marked "Author's Copy," "Publisher's Copy," "Printer's Copy," "Binder's
Copy," and "File Copy."

Note: An examined copy had the holograph poem "The White Wolves Follow
the Little Old Lady from Pasadena" bound in. An advertising flyer
designated "Broadside/Flyer No. 6," printing one poem from the book,
preceded publication. 100 copies were numbered and signed by the author.

A32   The Owl and the Snake   1973

Collation: Broadside; 19″ × 6 1/8″; printed on wove paper.

Publication: Published by the Perishable Press, Mt. Horeb, Wisconsin, in
1973. Edition size was 73 copies. Drawing by Ellen Lanyon.

Contents: "The Owl and the Snake."

A33   Still Life: Michael, Silver Flute and Violets   1973

Collation: Broadside; 14″ × 10″; printed on wove paper.

Publication: Published by the University of Connecticut, Storrs, in 1973. "Issued in an edition of 250 copies on the occasion of a reading by the poet at the University of Connecticut Library, November 6, 1973."

Contents: "Still Life: Michael, Silver Flute and Violets."

A34   Winter Sequences   1973

[no title page; on front cover, within partial frame ornamented with fruits and grains, in blue:] Diane Wakoski / [in red:] WINTER / SEQUENCES / [in blue:] A NEW YEAR'S GREETING / FROM THE / BLACK SPAR-ROW PRESS

Collation: Broadside, 18″ × 12″, folded twice to 9″ × 6 1/4″; folded into red wrappers and pasted to verso of front cover; printed in black and red on white wove paper. Colophon, from verso of front cover, printed in black: [publisher's emblem] / Design by Barbara Martin. Printed December 1973 as a / New Year's Greeting for the friends of the Black Sparrow / Press. One Hundred + twenty-six copies of this edition / have been numbered and signed by the author.

Publication: Published by the Black Sparrow Press, Los Angeles, California, 26 December 1973, for distribution gratis. Edition size was 626 copies. 100 copies were numbered 1-100 and signed; 26 copies were lettered A–Z and signed.

Contents: "Winter Sequences."

A35   Abalone   1974

(a) *First edition*:

[in red, and with ornamental first letter:] ABALONE / [in orange:] Diane Wakoski / [in black:] Black Sparrow Press [centered dot] Los Angeles / 1974

Collation: pp. [1–8]; 8 1/4″ × 4 7/8″; printed on wove paper.

Pagination: p. [1] title page, p. [2] copyright, pp. [3–7] text, p. [8] colophon: "Design by Barbara Martin. / Printed December 1974 as a / New Year's Greeting for the / friends of the Black Sparrow Press. / One hundred & twenty-six copies / of this edition have been / handbound in boards & numbered / & signed by the poet."

Binding: Issued in white paper wrappers. Front: [design in orange and green of vertical vine with foliage divides cover; to left, in dark green:] A / YEAR'S / END / POEM / FROM / THE / BLACK / SPARROW / PRESS / 1974. [to right, in orange:] A / YEAR'S / END / POEM / FROM / THE / BLACK / SPARROW / PRESS / 1975. Yellow flyleaves. Sewn with tie inside.

Publication: Published by the Black Sparrow Press, Los Angeles, 30 December 1974. Edition size was 500 copies.

Contents: "Abalone."

(b) *Limited edition*:   1974

Title page, Collation, & Pagination as A35 a.

Binding: Issued in white boards printed as wrappered issue. Yellow endsheets.

Dust jacket: Issued in a stiff white unprinted dust jacket.

Publication: Published by the Black Sparrow Press, Los Angeles, 30 December 1974. Edition size, according to the publisher, was "101 signed copies, of which 100 copies were numbered 1–100, and 1 copy marked 'File Copy.'"

(c) *Variant edition*:   1974

Title page, Collation, Pagination, Binding, Dust jacket, & Publication as A35 b, save 31 signed copies issued with red endsheets. 26 were lettered A–Z and 5 were author, publisher, printer, binder, and file copies, so marked.

A36   The Liar   1974

Collation: Broadside; 16″ × 21″; printed on wove paper.

Publication: Published by the Burning Deck Press, Providence, Rhode Island, in 1974. Edition size was 200 numbered copies. Illustration by Linda Lutes.

Contents: "The Liar."

A37   Marriage Poem   1974

(a) *First edition*:

Collation: Broadside; 8 1/2″ × 11″; printed on both yellow and grey wove paper. Italic title.

Publication: Published by the Old Marble Press, Ann Arbor, Michigan, in 1973. Size of the edition is unknown.

Contents: "Marriage Poem."

(b) *Limited edition*:

Publication as A37 a, but with Roman title on imitation vellum and measures 11″ × 17″. Size of edition unknown.

A38   Trilogy   1974

(a) *First edition*:

[in black:] DIANE WAKOSKI / [in heavy black print:] TRILOGY / [device] / COINS & COFFINS / DISCREPANCIES AND APPARI-TIONS / THE GEORGE WASHINGTON POEMS / 1974 / Doubleday & Company, Inc. / Garden City, New York

Collation: pp. [i–xiii] xiv–xvi [1–4] 5–29 [30–34] 35–108 [109–112] 113–166 [167–172]; 8 1/4″ × 5 1/2″; printed on wove paper.

Pagination: p. [1] half-title, p. [ii] blank, p. [iii] books by DW, p. [iv] blank, p. [v] title page, p. [vi] copyright, pp. [vii–xi] contents, p. [xii] blank, pp. [xiii]–xvi introduction, p. [1] half-title, p. [2] blank, p. [3] dedication, p. [4] blank, pp. 5–29 text, p. [30] blank, p. [31] half-title, p. [32] blank, p. [33] dedication, p. [34] blank, pp. 35–108 text, p. [109] half-title, p. [110] blank, p. [111] dedication, p. [112] blank, pp. 113–166 text, pp. [167–172] blank.

Binding: Bound in half black cloth with blue cloth over boards. Spine, reading downward, stamped in gold: DIANE WAKOSKI/TRILOGY/ Doubleday. Blue endpapers.

Dust jacket: Issued in white paper wrappers. Front: [photograph of sea shell and, in red:] Trilogy / [in black:] Diane Wakoski. Spine, reading downward: [in red:] Trilogy / [in black:] Diane Wakoski / [in black across bottom of spine:] Doubleday. Flaps: publisher's notes on DW, with price on front.

Publication: Published by Doubleday, Garden City, New York, in 1974 at $6.95.

Contents: Reprints *Coins & Coffins*, *Discrepancies and Apparitions*, and *The George Washington Poems*.

(b) *First paper edition*:   1974

Title page, *Collation*, *Pagination*, & *Contents* as A38 a.

Binding: Issued in stiff paper covers. Front: as A38 a. Back cover: note on DW and price. Spine, reading downward: [in red:] Trilogy / [in black:] Diane Wakoski / Doubleday.

Publication: Published by Doubleday in 1974 at $2.95.

A39   The Wandering Tattler   1974

(a) *First edition*:

[double spread, in pale yellow:] The Wandering Tattler [in green:] Poems by Diane Wakoski [slash] Illustrations by Ellen Lanyon / [illustration: birds, snake, and camel] / [in black:] Published as Our Sun enters Aries or [sic] the First Day of Spring 1974 The Perishable Press Limited, Driftless Wisconsin

Collation: pp. [1–36]; 13″ × 7″; printed on wove paper of various colors.

Pagination: p. [1] [reproduces, double spread with endsheet, the Lanyon illustration], p. [2] blank, p. [3] half-title, pp. [4–5] title, p. [6] copyright, p. [7] dedication, p. [8] illustration, p. [9] text, p. [10] blank, p. [11] text and illustration, pp. [12–13] illustration, with text at right, p. [14] blank, p. [15] text and illustration, pp. [16–17] text and illustration, p. [18] illustration, p. [19] text, p. [20] illustration, p. [21] text, p. [22] illustration, p. [23] text, p. [24] illustration, p. [25] text, p. [26] blank, p. [27] text and illustration, p. [28] blank, p. [29] [gold foil seal pasted on] colophon: "One hundred thirty copies, ten of which are on pure white and narrower," p. [30] blank, p. [31] publisher's note: "this whole page set aside mostly for visual resting and quiet reflection," pp. [32–33] [reproduces title page illustration], pp. [34–35] blank, p. [36] [reproduces, double spread with endsheet, the title page illustration].

Binding: Black cloth over boards with blue leather spine. Stamped on spine in gold: The Wandering Tattler [slash] Diane Wakoski. Issued in a slipcover of black cloth covered cardboard.

Publication: Published by the Perishable Press, Driftless, Wisconsin, in 1974. Edition size was 115 copies, signed by the author and numbered.

Contents: 9 "On Seeing Two Goldfinches," 11 "When the Quetzal Bird Stole Roadrunner's Feathers," 13 "Vulture Weather," 15 "The Owl & The Snake, A Fable," 16 "The Purple Finch Song," 19 "Looking for the Bald Eagle in Wisconsin," 27 "The Wandering Tattler."

(b) *Variant binding*:   1974

Title page, Collation, Pagination, Binding, & Contents as A39 a, save issued with a green leather spine.

Publication: Published by the Perishable Press, Driftless, Wisconsin, in 1974. 5 copies were issued with a green leather spine. Numbered and signed.

(c) *Limited edition*:   1974

Title page, Collation, Pagination, Binding, & Contents as A39 a, save measures 13″ × 6 1/2″ and printed on pure white paper. Blue leather spine.

Publication: Published by the Perishable Press, Driftless, Wisconsin, in 1974. 10 copies were issued in this format, numbered and signed.

Note: A39 a, A39 b, and A39 c are numbered in the same series, 1–130. The copy numbered 1 is an unsewn proof copy. A flyer, 13 1/4″ × 6 3/8″ on buff paper, preceded publication: "Easily, this is the most sumptuous book so far issued from this press and well worth all the waiting for." The flyer advertises 90 copies at a prepublication price of $125.00, with a price of $150.00 "after Easter."

A40   The Wisteria Promises   1974

Collation: Postcard; 5 1/8″ × 6 3/4″; printed on wove pink paper. Illustration by Rochelle Holt.

Publication: Published by the Cold Mountain Press, Austin, Texas, in 1974. Cold Mountain Press Poetry Post Card Series II, Number 6. Edition size unknown.

Contents: "The Wisteria Promises."

A41   Diane Wakoski / 2 Broadsides, 3 Postcards   1975

Collation: Portfolio; 13" × 14" brown folder.

Publication: Published by the Burning Deck Press, Providence, Rhode Island, in 1975. Size of the edition is unknown.

Contents: "Claws," "A Lover Disregards Names," "Comparisons," "Sometimes a Poet Will Hijack the Moon," "Love, the Lizard."

Note: Gathers postcards and broadsides published by the Burning Deck Press in 1972, 1973, and 1975. Each is described, in entries A23, A24, A29, and A28, respectively, with the exception of "Love, the Lizard."

A42   The Fable of the Lion and the Scorpion   1975

(a) *First edition*:

[left of page, in black:] THE / FABLE / OF / THE / LION / & / THE / SCORPION [right of page, in black:] Diane Wakoski / [illustration: flowers]

Collation: pp. [1–8]; 8 1/2" × 5 1/4"; printed on tan laid paper.

Pagination: p. [1] title page, p. [2] copyright and colophon: "1000 copies of this chapbook have been published. / 100 are hand-sewn, numbered & signed / by the poet in Madison, Wisconsin, / September, 1975," p. [3] dedication, p. [4] blank, pp. [5–7] text, p. [8] publications of the Pentagram Press.

Binding: Issued in stapled tan paper covers. Cover, top left and slanting to right: [in black:] THE / FABLE / OF / THE / LION / & / THE / SCOR-PION / DIANE WAKOSKI / [two ornamental rules]. Back cover: [in black:] $1.00 [slash] 3.00 signed / [two ornamental rules].

Publication: Published by the Pentagram Press, Milwaukee, Wisconsin, in 1975 at $1.00. Edition size was 900 copies.

Contents: "The Fable of the Lion and the Scorpion."

(b) *Limited edition*:   1975

Title page, Collation, Pagination, & Binding as A42 a, but sewn with tie inside.

Publication: Published by the Pentagram Press, Milwaukee, Wisconsin, in 1975 at $3.00. Edition size was 100 numbered copies, signed by the author.

A43   Virtuoso Literature for Two and Four Hands   1975

(a) *First edition*:

[in black:] DIANE WAKOSKI / Virtuoso / Literature / for Two / and Four / Hands / Doubleday & Company, Inc. / Garden City, New York / 1975

Collation: pp. [i–viii] ix–x, 1–85 [86]; printed on wove paper.

Pagination: p. [i] half-title, p. [ii] works by DW, p. [iii] title page, p. [iv] copyright, p. [v] dedication: "this book is dedicated to the snake in the garden, for he offered the taste of knowledge, without which I would rather not live," p. [vi] blank, p. [vii] preface, p. [viii] blank, pp. ix–x contents, pp. 1–85 text, p. [86] blank.

Binding: Bound in half grey cloth with red paper over boards. Spine, reading downward: [in red:] DIANE WAKOSKI Virtuoso Literature for Two and Four Hands Doubleday. White flyleaves.

Dust jacket: Issued in a white paper dust jacket. Front: [within white rule frame, in white:] Virtuoso / literature / for two / and four / hands / [white rule] / [in white:] new poems by / Diane / Wakoski. Front cover photograph by Alex Gotfryd. Back cover: photograph of DW by Thomas Victor. Spine, reading downward: [in black:] Virtuoso literature for two and four hands / Diane Wakoski / Doubleday. Flaps: publisher's note on DW.

Publication: Published by Doubleday, Garden City, New York, in 1975 at $4.95.

Contents: 1 "Pools of the Bright and Irradiating Sun," 3 "The Story of Richard Maxfield," 8 "Second Chance," 13 "Virtuoso Literature for Two and Four Hands," 21 "The Woman Who Tap-danced," 22 "Offering to Trade Lives with the Clam," 23 "The Neighbor's Cat," 24 "Poem Beginning With a Line from a Zebra," 25 "Story," 27 "The Bouquet," 30 "Cobra Lilies in the Super-market," 33 "The Emerald Essay," 43 "Still Life: Michael R., Silver Flute

and Violets," 45 "The Inevitable Garden," 48 "Walking Past Paul
Blackburn's Apt. on 7th St.," 50 "A Poem With a Blackburnian Warbler's
Beginning," 53 "Tango-ing," 56 "Winter Sequences," 61 "The Beautiful
Amanita Muscaria," 64 "Driving Gloves," 71 "Backing Up, or Tearing Up the
Garden Next to the Driveway," 73 "To the Young Man Who Left the
Flowers On My Desk One April Afternoon," 75 "A Drab Beach Reminds Me
of a Crippled Woman," 76 "Thorny Trunks," 78 "On Seeing Two Gold-
finches Fly Out of an Alder Tree, The Way You Are Swiftly Flying Out of
My Life," 80 "Blessing Ode for a Man With Fishbones Around His Neck,"
82 "Alone, Like a Window Washer at the 50th Story," 84 "Buds."

(b) *First paper edition*:   1975

Title page, Collation, Pagination, & Contents as A43 a.

Binding: Issued in white paper covers printed as hardcover edition, save with
photo credits, publisher's note on DW and price printed over photograph on
back cover.

Publication: Published by Doubleday, Garden City, New York, in 1975 at
$2.95.

Note: An advertising flyer printing "The Liar" and biographical information
preceded publication.

A44   George Washington's Camp Cups   1976

(*See photo page 49.*)

[in green:] Diane Wakoski / [reproduction of George Washington's signature
and, in black:] 'S / Camp Cups / The Red Ozier Press [slash] Madison

Collation: pp. [1–16]; 9″ × 6″; printed on wove paper.

Pagination: pp. [1–2] blank, p. [3] half-title, p. [4] printed illustration: George
Washington, p. [5] title page, p. [6] copyright, pp. [7–11] text, p. [12] blank,
p. [13] publisher's note, pp. [14–16] blank.

Binding: Issued in grey paper covers. On front cover, embossed: Diane
Wakoski / gwcc. Sewn with tie outside. Grey flyleaves.

Title page of George Washington's Camp Cups.

Publication: Published by the Red Ozier Press, Madison, Wisconsin, in 1976. Edition size was 150 copies, 50 of which were ". . .for the author & friends of the press."

Contents: "George Washington's Camp Cups."

Note: An examined author's copy had red flyleaves.

A45   Icicle Branches Breaking into Light: Selections from the Poetry   1976?

Note: Unexamined. Only one copy of this publication could be found. It is in the library of St. Andrews Presbyterian College, Laurinburg, North Carolina. St. Andrews was unwilling to loan its copy for examination. This book was produced by Margaret Wilson, a student at St. Andrews, under the aegis of the Curveship Press. 20 copies were printed.

A46   The Laguna Contract   1976

[in green:] THE / LAGUNA / CONTRACT / [in blue:] of diane wakoski / with illustrations and form / from the crepuscular press / printing through the meltwater and maple sap flow of wisconsin, this april of 1976

Collation: pp. [1–30]; 7″ × 8″; printed on various types and sizes of paper.

Pagination: p. [1] dedication ("to m"), p. [2] [rule of letter m's crosses page], p. [3] title page, p. [4] copyright, p. [5] blank, p. [6] [line drawing], pp. [7–29] text with illustrations, p. [30] blank, p. [31] publisher's note, p. [32] blank.

Binding: Issued in light blue construction paper wrappers, 7″ × 21″, with book enfolded in center. Front: [in green:] the laguna contract. Sewn with tie inside. Grey flyleaves.

Publication: Published by the Crepuscular Press, Madison, Wisconsin, in July 1976. Edition size was 125 copies.

Contents: "The Laguna Contract."

Note: A flyer in advance of publication announced prices: "85 copies are tendered / modestly if ordered before the mum festival / i.e. 27.50 until oct. 1st. / but 35.00 thereafter." The flyer is printed on white paper, folded and with a cutout, and also with a piece of paper attached by a string and printed with an "afterthought." The flyer was enclosed in a white paper folder and issued in a green mailing envelope.

A47   The Ring   1976

(See photos pages 51 and 52.)

[within green rule frame, in blue:] THE / [green rule] / [in blue:] RING / [green rule] / [in green:] DIANE / [green rule] / [in green:] WAKOSKI / [beneath rule frame, in black:] Santa Barbara / Black Sparrow Press / 1977

Collation: pp. [1–24]; 10 1/2″ × 7 1/8″; printed on wove paper.

Pagination: pp. [1–2] blank, p. [3] title page, p. [4] copyright, p. [5] contents, p. [6] blank, p. [7] half-title, p. [8] blank, p. [9] text, p. [10] blank, pp. [11–17] text, p. [18] blank, pp. [19–21] text, p. [22] blank, p. [23] colophon: "Printed January 1977 in Santa Barbara for / the Black Sparrow Press by Mackintosh &

Book cover of The Ring.

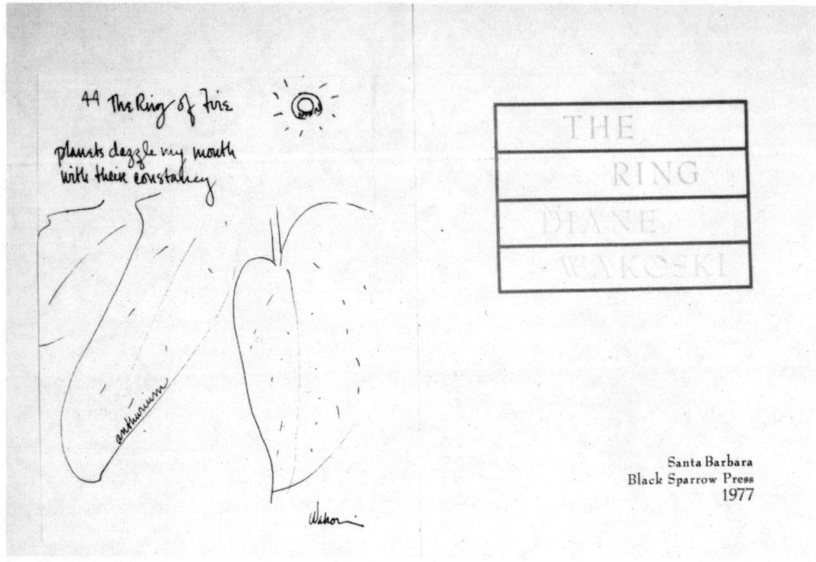

Title page of The Ring.

Young. / Design by Barbara Martin. This edition is / limited to 140 hard-cover copies numbered / & signed by the author; & 40 numbered copies / handbound in boards by Emily Paine, each / with an original ink drawing by Diane Wakoski," p. [24] blank.

Binding: Bound in half blue cloth with decorated blue paper over boards. Front: [within green rule frame, in light blue:] THE RING / [green rule] / [drawing by DW of potted plant] / [in light blue:] DIANE WAKOSKI. White paper label pasted on spine, reading downward: [in green:] THE RING [device] [in light blue:] Diane Wakoski. Purple endpapers.

Dust jacket: Issued in a clear acetate dust jacket.

Publication: Published by the Black Sparrow Press, Santa Barbara, California, 14 December 1976, at $25.00. Edition size was 146 signed copies. 140 copies were numbered 1–140. One copy was marked "File Copy" and five copies were marked "Author's Copy."

Contents: 9 "The Ring," 11 "Tearing Up My Mother's Letters," 13 "Deat T-," 19 "The Hitchhikers."

(b) *Limited edition:*   1976

Title page, Collation, Pagination, Dust jacket, & *Contents* as A47 a, save bound in half red cloth, instead of half blue cloth, and with an original signed ink drawing by DW tipped in facing the title page.

Publication: Published by the Black Sparrow Press, Santa Barbara, California, 14 December 1976, at $40.00. Edition size was 49 signed copies. 40 copies were numbered 1–40. One copy each was marked "Publisher's Copy," "Printer's Copy," "Binder's Copy," and "File Copy." Five copies were marked "Author's Copy."

A48   Waiting for the King of Spain   1976

(a) *First edition:*

[double spread, within rule frame which is blue on left page and green on right page, in green:] WAITING FOR THE [in blue:] KING OF SPAIN / [in yellow:] Diane Wakoski / [in black:] *Santa Barbara* / BLACK SPARROW PRESS / 1976

Collation: pp. [1–12] 13–46 [47–48] 49–71 [72–74] 75–92 [93–94] 95–117 [118–120] 121–134 [135–136] 137–157 [158–164]; 8 7/8″ × 5 7/8″; printed on wove paper.

Pagination: p. [1] books by DW, pp. [2–3] title page, p. [4] copyright, p. [5] dedication, p. [6] blank, pp. [7–9] table of contents, p. [10] epigraph, p. [11] half-title, p. [12] blank, pp. 13–[48] text, p. 49 blank, pp. 50–71 text, p. [72] blank, p. [73] half-title, p. [74] blank, pp.75–[93] text, p. [94] blank, pp. 95–117 text, p. [118] blank, p. [119] half-title, p. [120] blank, pp. 121–[135] text, p. [136] blank, pp. 137–157 text, p. [158] blank, p. [159] colophon: "Printed October 1976 in Santa Barbara & Ann Arbor / for the Black Sparrow Press by Mackintosh & Young / and Edwards Brothers Inc. Design by Barbara Martin. / This edition is published in paper wrappers; there are / 500 hardcover trade copies; 250 hardcover copies / numbered & signed by the author; & 50 numbered copies / handbound in boards by Earle Gray, each containing an / original holograph poem by Diane Wakoski," p. [160] blank, p. [161] publisher's note on author's life and photograph of DW by Thomas Victor, pp. [162–164] blank.

Binding: Issued in cream paper wrappers. Front: [within green, yellow, and red ruled frames, with design of tree in yellow at left and right within frames, in blue:] WAITING / FOR / THE / KING / OF / SPAIN / [within device of scroll, in green:] Diane Wakoski. Spine, reading downward: [in green:] Diane Wakoski [in blue:] WAITING FOR THE KING OF SPAIN [in green:] Black Sparrow Press. Green flyleaves.

Publication: Published by the Black Sparrow Press, Santa Barbara, California, 29 November 1976, at $4.00. Edition size was 3016 copies.

Contents: 13 "Beyond the Trunks of the Palm Trees," 15 "Precisely, Not Violets," 18 "April Snow," 20 "A Shipment of George Washington Apples Arrives in a Snowstorm," 22 "Looking for the King of Spain," 24 "There Are Lions Like Yellow Dogs," 28 "The King of Spain Eschews the Freezer," 29 "Walking on the Beach at Laguna in the Morning With a Man Who Has a Gold Tooth," 31 "The Laguna Contract," 37 "Counting Your Blessings on All Six Fingers of Your Hand: A Vigil," 40 "Reminded of One of Those Girls I Never Was," 44 "Burning My Bridges Behind Me," 49 "George Washington Meets the King of Spain," 52 "Gold," 54 "Some Constantly Besieged Castle," 56 "Love Poem to Francis X. Osgood," 59 "The Fear of Dropping the Violin," 62 "The Pepper Plant," 70 "Empty Night, When You Hear the Surf Pounding," 75 "Not the Blood a Dreamer Kissed from My Mouth," 76 "The Dream," 78 "Water," 79 "Write," 81 "For Michael, Armoured With Roses," 82 "The Lady Who Sang," 83 "The Dark Clack of Morays," 84 "Light," 85 "Sun With Hands for Rays," 86 "Donna," 87 "The Roses Were Talking," 88 "Eat Your Rose Hips, C'est la Vie," 89 "Poetry, the Unpredictable, 91 "David," 92 "Western Music," 95 "Those Mythical Silver Pears," 97 "A Broken Season," 99 "Saying Goodbye to Someone You Were Just Getting Ready to Say Hello To," 101 "The Skier," 104 "Marriage Poem," 105 "The Wandering Tattler," 107 "Harry Moon from My Child's Anthology of Verse," 113 "Polish Love Poem for Dan Whose Last Name Is Harder to Pronounce Than Mine," 115 "The Tattooed Man Who Swallows Swords," 121 "Recognizing That My Wrists Always Have Salmon Leaping for Spring in Them," 124 "A Poem for the Man Who Drives the Sphinx and Makes All Ferrari Owners Weep with Envy," 126 "Bracelets," 127 "On the Subject of Roses," 128 "What the Struggle Is All About," 130 "Some Man," 132 "The Old Golden Fleece," 134 "In the Palm Of," 137 "Daugher Moon," 140 "Two," 141 "Ode to a Lebanese Crock of Olives," 144 "To the Thin and Elegant Woman Who Resides inside of Alix Nelson," 147 "Dear Debra," 149 "My Aunt Eva Who Collected More Than 5,000 Pairs of Salt and Pepper Shakers before Her Husband Told Her He Wouldn't Buy Any More Cabinets for Them," 151 "Describe the Sky on a Postcard," 152 "Sestina to the Common Glass of Beer: I Do Not Drink Beer," 154 "George Washington's Camp Cups."

(b) *Hardcover edition*:   1976

Title page, Collation, Pagination & Contents as A48 a, save measures 9″ × 6″.

Binding: Bound in half yellow cloth with white paper over boards. Front cover is printed as wrappered issue. White paper label pasted on spine: [in red:] Diane Wakoski / [in blue:] WAITING FOR THE KING OF SPAIN. Green endpapers.

Dust jacket: Issued in a clear acetate dust jacket.

Publication: Published by the Black Sparrow Press, Santa Barbara, California, 29 November 1976, at $10.00. Edition size was 500 copies.

(c) *Variant binding*:   1976

Title page, Collation, Pagination, Binding, Dust jacket, & Contents as A48 b, save bound in half orange cloth instead of half yellow cloth.

Publication: Published by the Black Sparrow Press, Santa Barbara, California, 29 November 1976, at $15.00. Edition size was 250 signed and numbered copies and one additional copy marked "File Copy," also signed.

(d) *Limited edition*:   1976

Title page, Collation, Pagination, Binding, Dust jacket, & Contents as A48 c, save bound in half multicolored cloth, instead of half orange cloth, and with an extra leaf bound in between pp. [4–5] for a holograph poem by the author.

Publication: Published by the Black Sparrow Press, Santa Barbara, California, 29 November 1976, at $30.00. Edition size was 55 signed copies. 50 copies were numbered 1–50. One copy each was marked "Author's Copy," "Publisher's Copy," "Printer's Copy," "Binder's Copy," and "File Copy."

Note: An examined copy had the holograph poem "The Key" bound in, as does the example in *A Bibliography of the Black Sparrow Press*.

**A49   Having Replaced Love with Food and Drink:
          A Poem for Those Who've Reached Forty**   1977

Collation: Broadside; 17 1/4″ × 11 3/4″.

Publication: Published by the A Poem a Month Club, Huntington, New York, in 1977; edition size unknown.

Contents: "Having Replaced Love."

A50   Overnight Projects with Wood   1977

[in blue:] Overnight Projects With Wood / [in green:] A poem by Diane Wakoski / [in blue:] The Red Ozier Press [slash] Madison. Printed over a collage illustration by Steve Miller.

Collation: pp. [1–16]; 4″ × 5″; printed on wove paper.

Pagination: pp. [1–2] blank, p. [3] half-title, p. [4] blank, p. [5] title page, p. [6] copyright, p. [7] text, p. [8] blank, p. [9] text, p. [10] blank, p. [11] text, p. [12] blank, p. [13] publisher's note, pp. [14–16] blank.

Binding: Issued in blue paper covers. Front: [in blue:] Overnight Projects With Wood [slash] Diane Wakoski. Sewn with tie outside.

Publication: Published by the Red Ozier Press, Madison, Wisconsin, in August 1977. Edition size was 170 copies.

Contents: "Overnight Projects With Wood."

Note: Covers vary in color. Both light blue and dark blue covers were issued. As well, two copies were examined which had grey paper covers.

A51   Spending Christmas with the Man
**   from Receiving at Sears**   1977

(a) *First edition*:

[in orange:] DIANE WAKOSKI / [within rounded orange rule frame, in green:] SPENDING / CHRISTMAS / WITH / THE / MAN / FROM / RECEIVING / AT / SEARS / [orange calligraphic rule] / [in black:] Black Sparrow Press [green dot] Santa Barbara [green dot] 1977

Collation: pp. [1–16]; 7 7/8″ × 4 3/4″; printed on wove paper.

Pagination: p. [1] title page, p. [2] copyright, p. [3] half-title, p. [4] blank, pp. [5–13] text, p. [14] blank, p. [15] colophon: [publisher's emblem] Published

December 1977 / as a Christmas Greeting / to the friends of the / Black Sparrow Press. / 176 copies of this edition / have been handbound in / boards + are numbered + signed by the author, p. [16] blank.

Binding: Issued in white paper wrappers. Front: [within rounded blue rule frame, and with ornamental first letter, in orange:] A YEAR'S / END / GREETING / FROM / THE / BLACK / SPARROW / PRESS / [in blue:] 1977. Sewn, with tie inside. Issued in a printed white mailing envelope.

Publication: Published by the Black Sparrow Press, Santa Barbara, California, 14 December 1977, for distribution gratis. Edition size was 300 copies.

Contents: "Spending Christmas with the Man from Receiving at Sears."

Note: According to the publisher, "The first issue with the author's name printed in orange on the title page resulted from a printer's error."

(b) *Second issue*:   1977

Title page, Collation, Pagination, & Binding as A51 a, save author's name on title page is printed in black, instead of orange. 515 copies.

(c) *Hardcover edition*:   1977

Title page, Collation, & Pagination A51 b.

Binding: Bound in half orange cloth with white paper over boards. Front cover: as wrappered issue. Orange flyleaves.

Dust jacket: Issued in an unprinted white paper dust jacket.

Publication: Published by the Black Sparrow Press, Santa Barbara, 14 December 1977, for distribution gratis. Edition size was 151 signed copies. 150 copies were numbered 1–150. One copy was marked "File Copy."

(d) *Limited edition*:   1977

Title page, Collation, Pagination, & Binding as A51 c, save bound in half multicolored cloth, instead of half orange cloth.

Dust jacket: Issued in an unprinted orange paper dust jacket.

Publication: Published by the Black Sparrow Press, Santa Barbara, California, 14 December 1977, for distribution gratis. Edition size was 31 signed

copies. 26 copies were lettered A–Z. One copy each was marked "Author's
Copy," "Publisher's Copy," "Printer's Copy," "Binder's Copy," and "File
Copy."

A52   The Man Who Shook Hands   1978

(a) *First edition*:

[in black:] The man / who shook / hands / DIANE WAKOSKI / Doubleday & Company, Inc. / Garden City, New York / 1978

Collation: pp. [1–6] 7–8 [9–12] 13–54 [55–56] 57–73 [74–76] 77–83 [84–86]
87–99 [100–102] 103–118 [119–120]; 8 1/8" × 5 1/2"; printed on wove paper.

Pagination: p. [1] half-title, p. [2] blank, p. [3] books by DW, p. [4] blank,
p. [5] title page, p. [6] copyright, pp. 7–8 contents, p. [9] introduction,
p. [10] blank, p. [11] "I The man / who shook / hands," p. [12] blank, pp. 13–54
text, p. [55] "II / Life is like / a game of cards," p. [56] blank, pp. 57–73 text,
p. [74] blank, p. [75] "III Extending the moon's / complicated geography,"
p. [76] blank, pp. 77–83 text, p. [84] blank, p. [85] "IV / Tributes and
transparencies," p. [86] blank, pp. 87–99 text, p. [100] blank, p. [101] "V /
The ring," p. [102] blank, pp. 103–118 text, pp. [119–120] blank.

Binding: Bound in half blue cloth with tan colored paper over boards.
Stamped in gold on spine, reading downward: DIANE WAKOSKI / The
man who shook hands / DOUBLEDAY. White flyleaves.

Dust jacket: Issued in white paper wrappers. Front: [in white:] The / man /
who / shook / hands / diane / wakoski. Photograph by Alex Gotfryd. Back:
excerpt from "The Hitchhikers." Spine, reading downward: [in black:] the
man who shook hands / diane wakoski / doubleday. Flaps: publisher's notes
on DW.

Publication: Published by Doubleday, Garden City, New York, in 1978 at
$6.95.

Contents: 13 "The Blue Swan, An Essay on Music," 31 "Running Men," 36
"Standing at the Door," 39 "Love Poem to Leon Edel & Ross MacDonald,"
43 "The King of Spain Discovered as a Mexican Bandit," 44 "Thinking of
Rilke's Mustache While Writing to the Man in Receiving at Sears," 48 "The
Photograph in the Letter," 50 "Overnight Projects with Wood," 53 "For the
Running Man," 57 "Life Is Like a Game of Cards, Etc.," 60 "How Do You
Tell a Story," 66 "A Poem in Response to Rexroth, Etc.," 70 "The Magician

without the Powers of the Sun," 72 "A Valentine for Ben Franklin Who Drives a Truck in California," 77 "Looking for the Bald Eagles in Wisconsin," 87 "The Last Poem of the Year, Written in an Airport," 92 "The Pumpkin Pie," 103 "The Ring," 105 "Tearing Up My Mother's Letters," 107 "Letter to T-," 110 "Gladiolas," 112 "The Hitchhikers," 115 "Views," 117 "The Photos."

(b) *First paper edition*:   1978

Title page, Collation, Pagination, & Contents as A52 a.

Binding: Issued in stiff white paper covers which reproduce dust jacket of hardcover edition with photo credit, price, etc. added to back cover. Spine, reading downward: [in black:] THE MAN WHO SHOOK HANDS / DIANE WAKOSKI / DOUBLEDAY.

Publication: Published by Doubleday, Garden City, New York, in 1978 at $3.95.

A53   Trophies   1979

Title page: Printed over reproduction of DW's watercolor of butterfly. [in blue:] Diane Wakoski / [in orange:] TROPHIES / [in blue:] Black Sparrow Press - Santa Barbara - 1979

Collation: pp. [1–8] 9–11 [12] 13–15 [16] 17–19 [20] 21–25 [26–28]; 10 3/4″ × 7 1/2″; printed on wove paper.

Pagination: pp. [1–2] blank, p. [3] title page, p. [4] copyright, acknowledgments, p. [5] table of contents, p. [6] blank, p. [7] half-title, p. [8] blank, pp. 9–11 text, p. [12] blank, pp. 13–15 text, p. [16] blank, pp. 17–19 text, p. [20] blank, pp. 21–25 text, p. [26] blank, p. [27] colophon: "Printed October 1979 in Santa Barbara for the / Black Sparrow Press by Mackintosh & Young. / Design by Barbara Martin. This edition is / limited to 200 hardcover copies numbered & / signed by the author; & 50 numbered copies / handbound in boards by Earle Gray, each / with an original watercolor by Diane Wakoski," p. [28] blank.

Binding: Bound in half blue cloth with tan boards. Front: [inside orange rectangle, in white:] DIANE WAKOSKI / [inside orange rectangle, in blue:] TROPHIES / [inside orange rectangle: reproduction of author's watercolor of butterfly in yellow, blue and black]. Tan paper label pasted on spine: [in blue:] TROPHIES [device] [in orange:] DIANE WAKOSKI. Orange endpapers and white flyleaves. As noted in the colophon, 50 copies have an original watercolor tipped in.

Dust jacket: Issued in a clear acetate jacket.

Publication: Published by the Black Sparrow Press, Santa Barbara, California, in 1979; edition size 250 copies.

Contents: 9 "Pamela's Green Tomato Pie," 13 "Measuring," 17 "Nell's Birthday," 21 "Trophies," 23 "What I Learned About the World from Barry Lopez."

A54   Cap of Darkness   1980

(a) *First edition*:

[within yellow rule frame, in blue:] DIANE WAKOSKI / [within yellow rule frame, in black:] CAP OF / DARKNESS / Including / Looking for the King of Spain / & / Pachelbel's Canon / [at bottom of page, in black:] BLACK SPARROW PRESS / Santa Barbara - 1980

Collation: pp. [1–12] 13–27 [28–30] 31–117 [118–124]; 9″ × 5 3/4″; printed on wove paper.

Pagination: p. [1] other books by DW, p. [2] blank, p. [3] title page, p. [4] copyright and acknowledgment, p. [5] dedication ("TO THE MEMORY OF ROBINSON JEFFERS"), p. [6] blank, pp. [7–8] contents, p. [9] half-title, p. [10] blank, p. [11] preface, p. [12] blank, pp. 13–27 preface [three poems], p. [28] blank, p. [29] half-title, p. [30] blank, pp. 31–117 text, p. [118] blank, p. [119] colophon: "Printed February 1980 in Santa Barbara & Ann Arbor for the / Black Sparrow Press by Mackintosh and Young & Edwards / Brothers Inc. Design by Barbara Martin. This edition is / published in paper wrappers; there are 750 hardcover trade / copies; 250 hardcover copies have been numbered & signed by / the author; & 50 numbered copies have been handbound in / boards by Earle Gray each containing an original holograph / poem by Diane Wakoski," p. [120] blank. p. [121] photograph of DW by Robert Turney and publisher's note on DW, pp. [122–124] blank.

Binding: Issued in tangerine paper covers. Front: [in blue:] CAP OF / Darkness / [design of black, blue, and yellow squares] / [in yellow:] DIANE [superimposed, in black:] WAKOSKI. Spine: [in black:] DIANE WAKOSKI / [in blue:] CAP OF DARKNESS / [in black:] Black Sparrow Press.

Publication: Published by the Black Sparrow Press, Santa Barbara, California, in 1980 at $6.00.

Contents: 13 "Dear Michael," 16 "Whistling," 17 "Telling You True, About My Fantasy Life (For M.W.)," 21 "Discovering Michael As the King of Spain," 24 "Touching the King of Spain Underwater," 26 "In Praise of Modern Times," 31 "Spending the New Year With the Man from Receiving at Sears," 34 "A Dissertation on Smallness," 40 "Having Replaced Love With Food & Drink (A Poem for Those Who've Reached 40)," 41 "Precision," 44 "Pamela's Green Tomato Pie," 47 "Red Runner," 49 "Red Runner, Again," 50 "Not Breaking the Silence," 51 "Silver," 52 "Aging," 53 "White (To Norman Hindley)," 55 "Cap of Darkness," 58 "Lady's Slipper," 59 "Calla Lily," 61 "Nell's Birthday," 64 "Directions," 66 "Memory," 68 "Adventures on a Balcony Overlooking the Morning Ocean," 69 "Measuring," 72 "Trophies," 74 "What I Learned about the World from Barry Lopez (for William Stafford)," 77 "A Californian Fights Against the Old New England Traditions (To Stanley Kunitz)," 79 "Civilization," 80 "Pachelbel's Canon," 83 "Washing & Ironing," 87 "Searching for the Canto Fermo," 91 "Abalone," 96 "She Takes the Scissors," 97 "A Letter from Unwritten (Greed, Part 10)," 100 "The Moth," 103 "I Dream of My Failures with Ed Dorn as Judge," 106 "Edges," 107 "Final Crystal," 109 "To Be Haunted," 110 "What Do You Do?", 111 "Petunias," 112 "Another Goldfinch Story," 113 "Rapunzel & The Coyote," 115 "My Mother's Milkman."

(b) *Hardcover edition*:   1980

Title page, Collation, Pagination, & *Contents* as A54 a.

Binding: As A54 a, save with half blue cloth and over boards. Tangerine paper label, pasted on spine, reading downward: [in black:] DIANE WAKOSKI [in blue:] CAP OF DARKNESS. Blue endpapers and fly-leaves.

Dust jacket: Issued in a clear acetate dust jacket.

Publication: Published by the Black Sparrow Press, Santa Barbara, California, in 1980. Edition size was 750 copies: 500 unsigned copies at $14.00 and 250 signed and numbered copies at $20.00.

(c) *Limited edition*:   1980

Title page, Collation, Pagination, Binding, Dust jacket & *Contents* as A54 b, save bound in half flower patterned black cloth, and with a holograph poem tipped in between pp. [4] and [5].

Publication: Published by the Black Sparrow Press, Santa Barbara, California, in 1980. Edition size was 50 copies.

Note: An examined copy had the holograph poem "To Kenneth Anger, February 1980" tipped in.

A55   Divers   1980

Collation: Broadsheet; 15 1/4" × 10 3/4"; printed in black on stiff white laid paper. The title is embossed, at left, reading upward. The author's name is printed below the title in blue. Issued in a light blue paper cover, 26" × 20", folded to 13" × 20". A dark blue wrapper, 11 1/4" × 15 1/2", pasted to the cover, holds the broadsheet. White paper label pasted on cover: [in light blue:] DIVERS / [in black:] DIANE WAKOSKI / Barbarian Press. White paper label pasted inside cover: [drawing of printing press and bear] / [in blue:] ALBION BROADSHEET FIVE: / SEPTEMBER 1980 / [black rule] / [in black:] Divers is published by Barbarian Press in an edition / of seventy-five copies, of which fifty are for sale. The / text was handset in Bembo, and printed on dampened / Barcham Green RWS Rough handmade paper. / The press used was a Hopkinson & Cope Super / Royal Albion made in 1850.

Publication: Published by the Barbarian Press, Mission, B.C., Canada, in September 1980. Edition size was 75 copies.

Contents: "Divers."

A56   The Managed World   1980

(a) *First edition*:

[in red:] THE MANAGED WORLD / by Diane Wakoski [slash] [in blue:] RED OZIER PRESS

Collation: pp. [1–16]; 6" × 4"; printed on laid paper.

Pagination: pp. [1–2] blank, p. [3] title page, p. [4] acknowledgment and copyright, pp. [5–8] text, p. [9] illustration, pp. [10–15] text, p. [16] colophon: [in blue:] TWO HUNDRED COPIES printed in Poliphilus types / (thank you Aldus & Pat Taylor; 1499–1980) / on Tidepool papers made with Dieu Donne Mill's help / before the sacrifice of the sheep in Tangier / and during the Harvest Moon above / Warren Street in New York City / Fifteen copies are hardbound / .

Binding: Issued in a grey paper folded wrapper. The wrapper is embossed with a design of butterflies. Sewn with white string. Grey flyleaves.

Publication: Published by the Red Ozier Press, Madison, Wisconsin, in 1980. Edition size was 185 copies.

Contents: 5 "Precision," 10 "The Moth," 13 "The Managed World."

(b) *Limited edition*:   1980

Title page, Collation, Pagination, & Contents as A56 a.

Binding: Bound in half blue leather with half brown paper over boards. Front cover: printed butterfly design. Spine, reading downward, in blue: THE MANAGED WORLD BY DIANE WAKOSKI. Grey endpapers.

Publication: Published by the Red Ozier Press, Madison, Wisconsin, in 1980. Edition size was 15 copies.

Note: An examined "Author's Copy" has the illustration on p. [9] hand colored by the artist.

A57   Toward a New Poetry   1980

[in black:] Toward / a New / Poetry / DIANE WAKOSKI / Ann Arbor The University of Michigan Press

Collation: pp. [i–v] vi [vii] viii–x [xi] xii [1–2] 3–119 [120–122] 123–142 [143–144] 145–180 [181–182] 183–209 [210–212] 213–335 [336]; 5 1/4″ × 8″; printed on wove paper.

Pagination: p. [i] half-title, p. [ii] "Poets on Poetry / Donald Hall, General Editor," p. [iii] title page, p. [iv] copyright, pp. [v]–vi acknowledgments, pp. [vii]–x preface, pp. [xi]–xii contents, p. [1] half-title, p. [2] blank, pp. 3–119 text, p. [120] blank, p. [121] half-title, p. [122] blank, pp. 123–142 text, p. [143] half-title, p. [144] blank, pp. 145–180 text, p. [181] half-title, p. [182] blank, pp. 183–209 text, p. [210] blank, p. [211] half-title, p. [212] blank, pp. 213–335 text, p. [336] blank.

Binding: Issued in grey paper covers. Front: [in black:] Poets on Poetry / [black rule] / [in white:] Toward / a New / Poetry / [in black:] DIANE WAKOSKI. Back cover: publisher's note and list of books in series. Spine, reading downward: [in black:] WAKOSKI [in white:] Toward a New Poetry. White flyleaves.

Publication: Published by the University of Michigan Press, Ann Arbor, in 1980 at $4.95.

Contents: 3 "On Sentimentality," 11 "A Tribute to Anais Nin," 21 "Form Is an Extension of Content: Second Lecture," 30 "Some Ideas about Art," 37 "The Emerald Essay," 45 "Little Magazines and Poetry Factions," 57 "The Vain and Superficial in the World of Poetry," 68 "So Much Misreading," 77 "How to Treat a Poet," 90 "Form Is an Extension of Content: First Lecture," 106 "Creating a Personal Mythology: Third Lecture," 123 "Variations on a Theme: An Essay on Revision," 145 "The Natural Community," 156 "Letter to the Finalists of the Walt Whitman First-Book Poetry Contest," 183 "Poetry as the Dialogue We All Hope Someone Is Listening To," 195 "The Blue Swan: An Essay on Music in Poetry," 213 "An Interview with Diane Wakoski: Conducted by Clair Healey," 239 "Diane Wakoski: Interviewed by Alan Goya," 257 "An Interview with Diane Wakoski: Conducted by Elaine Hoffman Baruch," 284 "A Conversation with Diane Wakoski: By Larry Smith," 299 "An Interview with Diane Wakoski: By Andrea Musher."

A58   Looking for Beethoven in Las Vegas   1981

[with ornamental rule of devices, in yellow-brown, at top, right, and bottom, in black:] MX [raised and in blue:] 1 / [in black:] Looking For Beethoven In Las Vegas / by Diane Wakoski from the Red Ozier Press

Collation: pp. [1–8]; 9 1/2″ × 5 1/2″; printed on wove paper, 2 sheets folded vertically.

Pagination: p. [1] title page, p. [2] blank, pp. [3–7] text, p. [8] colophon: "200 copies made by hand in New York City."

Binding: Folded into a stiff grey paper wrapper. Front: [in black:] MX[1] / Diane Wakoski.

Publication: Published by the Red Ozier Press, Madison, Wisconsin, in 1981. Edition size was 200 copies.

Contents: "Looking for Beethoven in Las Vegas."

A59   Making a Sacher Torte   1981

(*See photo page 65.*)

[on left of double spread title page, in black:] Making A Sacher Torte / nine poems, twelve illustrations / Diane Wakoski & Ellen Lanyon / [on right of

Making A Sacher Torte

nine poems, twelve illustrations
Diane Wakoski ⸱ Ellen Lanyon

HEREWITH PUBLISHED AS A SEQUEL
TO THE 1974 WANDERING TATTLER
BUT REPLACING BIRDS WITH FOOD,
COOKING, EATING AND DRINKING
IN THE SEASON OF HARVESTS & ALL
SAINTS DAY, PERRY TOWNSHIP NEAR

Contents :: 1 / Having Replaced Love With Food And Drink (a poem for
those who have reached forty); 2 / Breakfast; 3 / My Mother's Milkman;
4 / Making A Sacher Torte; 5 / Pamela's Green Tomato Pie; 6 / Saturday
Night (For Barbara Drake); 7 / Ode to a Lebanese Crock of Olives (For
Walter's Aunt Libby's diligence in making green olives); 8 / Sally Plum;
9 / Coprinus Comatus: Evening Mushrooms, Morning Milk :: copyright

by the perishable press limited / mount horeb 1981

MINOR CONFLUENCE / WISCONSIN

Title page for Making a Sacher Torte.

double spread title page, in black:] HEREWITH PUBLISHED AS A SE-
QUEL / TO THE 1974 WANDERING TATTLER / BUT REPLACING
BIRDS WITH FOOD, / COOKING, EATING AND DRINKING / IN
THE SEASON OF HARVESTS & ALL / SAINTS DAY, PERRY
TOWNSHIP NEAR / MINOR CONFLUENCE [slash] WISCONSIN /
[on left of double spread title page, in blue:] Contents:: 1 [slash] Having
Replaced Love With Food and Drink (a poem for / those who have reached
forty); 2 [slash] Breakfast; 3 [slash] My Mother's Milkman; / 4 [slash] Mak-
ing A Sacher Torte; 5 [slash] Pamela's Green Tomato Pie; 6 [slash] Saturday
/ Night (For Barbara Drake); 7 [slash] Ode to a Lebanese Crock of Olives
(for / Walter's Aunt Libby's diligence in making green olives); 8 [slash] Sally
Plum; / 9 [slash] Coprinus Comatus: Evening Mushrooms, Morning Milk::
Copyright / [in black:] by the perishable press limited [slash] mount horeb
1981

Collation: pp. [1–36]; 11" × 7 1/2"; printed on shadwell paper.

Pagination: p. [1] Ellen Lanyon illustration, double spread with endpaper, pp.
[2–3] title pages, pp. [4–5] Lanyon illustration, p. [6] ACKNOWLEDGE-
MENT [sic], p. [7] FOR THE FEAST LETTER GANG, p. [8] title,

"Having Replaced Love With Food And Drink," with Lanyon illustration, p. [9] text, p. [10] Lanyon illustration, pp. [11–15] text, p. [16] title, "Making a Sacher Torte," and Lanyon illustration, pp. [17–21] text, p. [22] illustration, pp. [23–27] text, p. [28] illustration, p. [29] text, p. [30] illustration, pp. [31–33] text, p. [34] blank, p. [35] POSTFACE [slash] COLOPHON / Our most discerning reader will have noticed by this point (with / deliquescing heart or intestines) egregious flaws encumbering the / edition. None were intended - of course but all production here is / without Royal Patent & so remains a continuing learning process / essentially among friends. These 2,500+ sheets of Shadwell paper / were "apprectice-formed" in the barn & printed undampened in / thirty-nine press-runs on the non-automatic Vandercook. This is / Sabon Antiqua type from Stempel & is composed slowly by hand / as were the poems. The edition is but 225 copies & you have N$^{\underline{o}}$ 21 /, pp. [36–40] blank.

Binding: Decorated black cloth over boards with grey leather spine. Embossed on spine, reading downward: DIANE WAKOSKI [centered dot] MAKING A SACHER TORTE. Light blue endpaper at front and blue endpaper at back.

Publication: Published by the Perishable Press, Mount Horeb, Wisconsin, in 1981. Edition size was 225 copies. A flyer in advance of publication offered 160 copies at a "prepublication retail price" of $180.00.

Contents: 8 "Having Replaced Love with Food and Drink," 13 "My Mother's Milkman," 16 "Making a Sacher Torte," 20 "Pamela's Green Tomato Pie," 24 "Ode to a Lebanese Crock of Olives," 30 "Sally Plum," 32 "Coprinus Comatus: Evening Mushrooms, Morning Milk."

A60   Peaches   1981

Collation: Broadside; 13″ × 9 3/4″; printed on reddish-brown laid paper. Title above text in yellow. Colophon: "This broadside was printed at The / Toothpaste Press for Bookslinger on / the occasion of the author's reading at / Walker Art Center, February 26, / 1981. © 1981 by Diane Wakoski. / The edition consists of 85 numbered / & signed copies. This is   ."

Publication: Published by the Walker Art Center/Bookslinger, St. Paul, Minnesota, in 1981.

Contents: "Peaches."

Note: An unknown number of copies were gathered in *20 Broadsides*, a portfolio issued by the Walker Art Center.

A61   The Magician's Feastletters   1982

(a) *First edition*:

[in black:] DIANE WAKOSKI / [silver rule] / [in black:] THE MAGI-
CIAN'S / FEASTLETTERS / [design in red] / BLACK SPARROW
PRESS / SANTA BARBARA - 1982

Collation: pp. [i–ii] [1–10] 11–33 [34–36] 37–74 [75–76] 77–92 [93–94] 95–119
[120–122] 123–129 [130–136]; 9″ × 6″; printed on wove paper.

Pagination: p. [i] "ALSO BY DIANE WAKOSKI," p. [ii] blank, p. [1] title
page, p. [2] copyright and acknowledgments, pp. [3–4] blank, p. [5] half-
title and epigraph, p. [6] blank, pp. [7–8] contents, p. [9] "AUTUMN," p.
[10] blank, pp. 11–33 text, p. [34] blank, p. [35] "WINTER," p. [36] blank,
pp. 37–74 text, p. [75] "SPRING," p. [76] blank, pp. 77–92 text, p. [93]
"SUMMER," p. [94] blank, pp. 95–119 text, p. [120] blank, p. [121] "EN-
VOI," p. [122] blank, pp. 123–129 text, p. [130] blank, p. [131] colophon:
[publisher's device] / [in black:] Printed February 1982 in Santa Barbara &
Ann Arbor / for the Black Sparrow Press by Graham Mackintosh / & Edwards Brothers Inc. Design by Barbara Martin. / This edition is published
in paper wrappers; / there are 750 hardcover trade copies; 250 copies / have
been numbered & signed by the author; & / 50 numbered copies have been
handbound in boards / by Earle Gray each containing an original holograph /
poem by Diane Wakoski. /, p. [132] publisher's note on the author, p. [133]
Robert Turney photograph of DW, pp. [134–136] blank.

Binding: Issued in wrappers printed with design in yellow, red, blue, and
silver. Front cover, amid design and in black: DIANE WAKOSKI / THE
MAGICIAN'S / FEASTLETTERS /. Yellow paper label pasted on spine,
reading downward and in black: Diane Wakoski THE MAGICIAN'S
FEASTLETTERS. Red flyleaves.

Publication: Published by the Black Sparrow Press, Santa Barbara, California, in 1982 at $6.00.

Contents: 11 "Breakfast," 14 "Divers," 16 "Coprinus Comatus: Evening
Mushrooms, Morning Milk," 18 "The Boy Magicians," 30 "Un Morceau en
Forme de Poire," 37 "Molokai," 42 "Making a Sacher Torte," 47 "Little
Tricks of Linear B," 56 "Sally Plum," 58 "The Ice Queen's Calla Lily
Fingers," 60 "Paleolithic," 61 "Jekyl Island," 63 "L'Enfant Terrible," 64
"Human History: Its Documents," 67 "Wrenching Grace," 68 "The Dark
Procession," 71 "The Dark Procession, Reviewed," 77 "Frog Mozart," 80
"Green Thumb," 87 "Saturday Night," 90 "White Gloves, White Feet,"

95 "Orphée," 97 "Leaving Waterloo," 100 "The Frame," 102 "Eleanor on the Cliff," 107 "Whole Sum," 109 "Morning Thunderstorm," 111 "Sailor's Daughter," 113 "Peaches," 114 "Gardenias," 117 "For Clint on the Desert," 123 "A Letter to Wang Wei on the Season of Tumultuous Magicians," 126 "Why I Am Not a Painter."

(b) *Hardcover edition*:   1982

Title page, Collation, Pagination, Binding, & *Contents* as A61 a, save with half orange cloth over boards.

Dust jacket: Issued in a clear acetate dust jacket.

Publication: Published by the Black Sparrow Press, Santa Barbara, California, in 1982 at $14.00. Edition size was 750 copies.

(c) *Limited edition*:   1982

Title page, Collation, Pagination, Binding, Dust jacket, & *Contents* as A61 b, save with half blue cloth instead of half orange cloth, and with a holograph poem tipped in between pp. [2] and [3].

Publication: Published by the Black Sparrow Press, Santa Barbara, California, in 1982. Edition size was 50 copies.

Note: An examined copy had "fragment from Letter to Wang Wei On The Season Of Tumultuous Magicians" tipped in (with "could" for "did" in line 12).

A62   The Lady Who Drove Me to the Airport   1982

(a) *First edition*:

[in black:] Diane Wakoski / [in green:] The Lady Who Drove / Me to the Airport / Metacom Press [raised dot] Worcester [raised dot] 1982

Collation: pp. [1–16]; 6″ × 4 3/4″; printed on laid paper.

Pagination: pp. [1–2] blank, p. [3] half-title, p. [4] blank, p. [5] title page, p. [6] copyright, "Metacom Limited Editions Series, No. 6," pp. [7–12] text, p. [13] blank, p. [14] colophon: "This first printing of / THE LADY WHO DROVE ME TO THE AIRPORT / is limited to 150 copies, numbered 1–150 and hand-sewn into / a soft French marble wrapper, and twenty-six hardbound / copies, lettered A–Z, which are not for sale. / All copies have been signed by the author. / The types are Centaur and Arrighi; the paper is Antique Laid. / Hand-sct, printed and bound / by Nancy King and William Ferguson, / March 1982 / , pp. [15–16] blank.

Binding: Issued in a multicolored marble paper wrapper. Tan paper label pasted on front cover: [in reddish-brown:] Diane Wakoski / The Lady Who Drove / Me to the Airport /. Sewn with tie inside. Tan flyleaves.

Publication: Published by the Metacom Press, Worcester, in March 1982, at $25.00. Edition size was 150 copies.

Contents: "The Lady Who Drove Me to the Airport."

(b) *Limited edition*:   1982

Title page, Collation, Pagination, & *Contents* as A62 a, save measures 4 1/2″ × 6″.

Binding: Bound in half purple cloth over boards with half purple and gold marbellized paper. Tan paper label pasted on spine: [in blue:] Diane Wakoski /. Tan endpapers and flyleaves.

Dust jacket: Issued in a clear acetate dust jacket.

Publication: Published by the Metacom Press, Worcester, in March, 1982. Edition size was 26 copies, lettered A–Z and signed by the author.

A63   Saturn's Rings   1982

[double-spread title page with embossed vertical rules forming a circle in center of pages; pink horizontal rule on left page; below pink rule on left page, in red:] DIANE WAKOSKI / [double-spread pink rule] / [double-spread in purple]: SATURN'S RINGS / [double-spread pink rule] / [on right page in red:] TARG EDITIONS / [pink rule]

Collation: pp. [i–iv] [1–5] 6 [7] 8 [9] 10 [11] 12 [13] 14 [15] 16 [17] 18 [19] 20 [21] 22 [23] 24 [25] 26 [27] 28 [29] 30 [31] 32 [33] 34 [35] 36 [37] 38 [39] 40 [41] 42 [43] 44 [45] 46 [47] 48 [49] 50 [51] 52 [53] 54 [55] 56 [57] 58 [59] 60 [61] 62 [63] 64 [65] 66 [67–72]; 7″ × 6 1/8″; printed on laid paper.

Pagination: pp. [i–iii] blank, pp. [iv–1] title pages, p. [2] copyright, p. [3] dedication: "To all those poets and friends who wear Saturn's Rings," pp. [4–5] contents, pp. 6–[7] introduction, p. 8 title, p. [9] text, p. 10 blank,

p. [11] text, p. 12 blank, p. [13] text, p. 14 title, p. [15] text, p. 16 blank, p. [17] text, p. 18 blank, p. [19] text, p. 20 title, p. [21] text, p. 22 blank, p. [23] text, p. 24 title, p. [25] text, p. 26 blank, p. [27] text, p. 28 blank, p. [29] text, p. 30 blank, p. [31] text, p. 32 blank, p. [33] text, p. 34 title, p. [35] text, p. 36 blank, p. [37] text, p. 38 blank, p. [39] text, p. 40 title, p. [41] text, p. 42 title, p. [43] text, p. 44 blank, p. [45] text, p. 46 title, p. [47] text, p. 48 blank, p. [49] text, p. 50 blank, p. [51] text, p. 52 blank, p. [53] text, p. 54 title, p. [55] text, p. 56 blank, p. [57] text, p. 58 title, p. [59] text, p. 60 blank, p. [61] text, p. 62 blank, p. [63] text, p. 64 blank, p. [65] text, p. 66 blank, p. [67] text, p. [68] blank, p. [69] colophon: "This first edition of SATURN'S RINGS, by Diane Wakoski, / is Number Fourteen of the Targ Editions, and is published / in April of 1982 in Greenwich Village, New York City. / . . . The edition is limited to 250 copies, signed by the author," pp. [70-72] blank.

Binding: Bound in half silver paper with half brown cloth over boards. Front cover: Robert Turney photograph of DW. Spine, reading downward, in silver: WAKOSKI SATURN'S RINGS [publisher's emblem]. Brown endpapers.

Dust jacket: Issued in an unprinted glassine dust jacket.

Publication: Published by Targ Editions, New York, in April 1982. Edition size was 250 signed copies.

Contents: 8 "The Ring of Irony," 14 "Sleeping in the Ring of Fire," 20 "For the Girl with Her Face in a Rose," 24 "Letter with the Ring of Truth," 34 "More Light, More Light," 40 "Saturn's Rings," 54 "Wakoski Visits Saturn," 58 "Joyce Carol Oates Plays the Saturn Piano."

A64   The Collected Greed, Parts 1–13   1984

(a) *First edition*:

[in red:] DIANE / WAKOSKI / [three double-spread rules, silver, green, and silver] / [in red:] THE COLLECTED / GREED / PARTS 1–13 / [two double-spread rules, green and silver] / [in red:] BLACK SPARROW PRESS / SANTA BARBARA — 1984

Collation: pp. [1–6] 7–9 [10–16] 17–22 [23–24] 25–34 [35–36] 37–43 [44–46] 47–55 [56–58] 59–70 [71–72] 73–81 [82–84] 85–93 [94–96] 97–103 [104–106] 107–119 [120–122] 123–124 [125–126] 127–141 [142–144] 145–226 [227–228] 229–248 [249–252]; 9″ × 5 7/8″; printed on wove paper.

Pagination: P. [1] books by DW, pp. [2–3] title pages, p. [4] copyright, p. [5] dedication: "for Robert," p. [6] blank, pp. 7–9 Preface, p. [10] blank, p. [11] contents, p. [12] blank, p. [13] half-title, p. [14] blank, p. [15] "GREED, Part 1," p. [16] blank, pp. 17–22 text, p. [23] "GREED, Part 2," p. [24] blank, pp. 25–34 text, p. [35] "GREED, Part 3," p. [36] blank, pp. 37–43 text, p. [44] blank, p. [45] "GREED, Part 4," p. [46] blank, pp. 47–55 text, p. [56] blank, p. [57] "GREED, Part 5," p. [58] blank, pp. 59–70 text, p. [71] "GREED, Part 6," p. [72] blank, pp. 73–81 text, p. [82] blank, p. [83] "GREED, Part 7," p. [84] blank, pp. 85–93 text, p. [94] blank, p. [95] "GREED, Part 8," p. [96] blank, pp. 97–103 text, p. [104] blank, p. [105] "GREED, Part 9," p. [106] blank, pp. 107–119 text, p. [120] blank, p. [121] "GREED, Part 10," p. [122] blank, pp. 123–124 text, p. [125] "GREED, Part 11," p. [126] blank, pp. 127–141 text, p. [142] blank, p. [143] "GREED, Part 12," p. [144] blank, pp. 145–226 text, p. [227] "GREED, Part 13," p. [228] blank, pp. 229–248 text, p. [249] colophon: "Printed May 1984 in Santa Barbara and Ann Arbor for the / Black Sparrow Press by Graham Mackintosh & Edwards Brothers, Inc. / Design by Barbara Martin. This edition is published in paper / wrappers; there are 300 hardcover trade copies; 200 hardcover / copies have been numbered & signed by the author; & 50 numbered / copies with an original holograph poem have been handbound in / boards by Earle Gray & are signed by Diane Wakoski," p. [250] photograph of DW by Robert Turney, p. [251] publisher's note on DW, p. [252] blank.

Binding: Issued in stiff grey paper wrappers. Front cover, half-framed by two vertical rules at left, silver and green, and by three rules at bottom, silver, green, and silver, double-spread to back cover: [in black:] THE COL-LECTED / [in red:] GREED / [in black:] PARTS 1–13 / [drawing, in black, of snake] / [in black:] DIANE / [in red:] WAKOSKI. Spine, reading downward: [in black:] DIANE WAKOSKI [in red:] THE COLLECTED GREED PARTS 1–13 [in black:] BLACK SPARROW PRESS [three rules, as described above]. Red flyleaves.

Publication: Published by the Black Sparrow Press, Santa Barbara, California, in 1984 at $10.00.

Contents: *Greed*, parts 1–9 and 11–13.

Note: In place of *Greed*, part 10, on pp. 123–124, is a note from the author to the reader. This section, it is explained, "will probably never be finished." However, ". . . I still retain the option in my mind to complete it someday. For that reason, I insist that the text of THE COLLECTED GREED: *Parts 1–13* not close its ranks, and that 'Part 10' be left open."

(b) *Hardcover edition*:   1984

Title page, Collation, Pagination, & Contents as A64 a.

Binding: Bound in grey paper over boards, printed as wrappered issue. White endpapers.

Publication: Published by the Black Sparrow Press, Santa Barbara, California, in May 1984 at $14.00. Edition size was 300 copies, 200 of which were numbered and signed by the author.

A65   A Snowy Winter in East Lansing   1985

Collation: Broadside; 13" × 9 3/8"; printed in black on white wove paper.

Publication: According to the colophon at the bottom of the sheet: "Designed and printed by J. Mudfoot for Table-Talk Press, Santa Barbara, California, in an edition of 100 signed copies." Published in December 1985.

Contents: "A Snowy Winter in East Lansing."

Note: The poem is printed in such a way as to fade from black, in the first stanza, to grey, in the last stanza.

**A66   Why My Mother Likes Liberace:
         A Musical Selection**   1985

(See photo page 73.)

(a) *First edition*:

[in black:] WHY MY MOTHER LIKES LIBERACE / A Musical Selection / DIANE WAKOSKI / with drawings by REBECCA GAVER / SUN LIZARD BOOK NUMBER ONE / TUCSON ARIZONA 1985 / [publisher's emblem] / SUN [centered dot] gemini Press

Collation: pp. [1–72]; 9" × 6"; printed on laid paper.

Pagination: pp. [1–2] blank, p. [3] epigraph: "*nothing is simple or innocent any more except poetry and music*," p. [4] drawing, p. [5] title page, p. [6] copyright, p. [7] dedication: "This book is for Robert, who has rhythm," p. [8] blank, p. [9] contents, p. [10] blank, p. [11] "Prelude," p. [12] drawing, pp. [13–17] text,

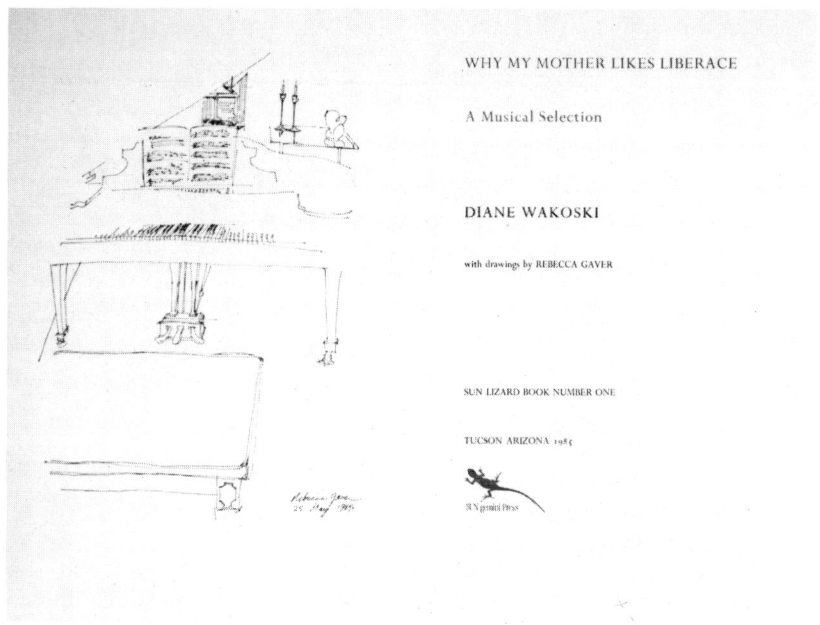

Title page of Why My Mother Likes Liberace.

p. [18] drawing, p. [19] text, p. [20] drawing, pp. [21–25] text, p. [26] drawing, pp. [27–39] text, p. [40] drawing, pp. [41–49] text, p. [50] drawing, pp.
[51–54] text, p. [55] drawing, pp. [56–59] text, p. [60] drawing, pp. [61–63]
text, p. [64] blank, pp. [65–66] acknowledgments, p. [67] blank, p. [68]
publisher's note on DW, p. [69] drawing of DW by Rebecca Gaver, p. [70]
blank, p. [71] colophon: "This book, the first from SUN/gemini Press, is
published by Clint / Colby with the assistance of John Hudak. The text was
set in 12 point / Perpetua by the Los Angeles Type Foundry. Display types
in Perpetua / and Spectrum were handset by Charles Alexander. A fine press
edition / of 125 copies has been printed by Chax Press, Tucson, and bound
by / Katherine Kuehn, Madison. The book has been designed by Nancy /
Solomon and Charles Alexander. This offset edition of 1000 copies / has been
printed in Tucson by Fabe Litho Ltd. on Kilmory text / and Lusterkote
cover papers, and has been bound in Phoenix by the / Roswell Bindery," p.
[72] blank.

Binding: Issued in stiff white paper covers. Front: [in black:] WHY MY
MOTHER LIKES LIBERACE / A Musical Selection / DIANE
WAKOSKI. Front cover drawing of piano by Rebecca Gaver. Back cover:
publisher's emblem in grey, ISBN numbers and price in black. Price: $5.95.

Spine, reading downward: [in black:] Diane Wakoski [abstract design] Why My Mother Likes Liberace.

Publication: Published by the SUN/gemini Press, Tucson, Arizona, in 1985 at $5.95. Edition size was 1138 copies.

Contents: 13 "The Piano," 14 "In Gratitude to Beethoven," 19 "Speonk Because It's a Favorite Word," 21 "Thanking My Mother for Piano Lessons," 27 "Virtuoso Literature for Two and Four Hands," 35 "Still Life: Michael R., Silver Flute and Violets," 37 "The Beautiful *Amanita Muscaria*," 41 "The Photograph in the Letter," 43 "The Dark Procession," 46 "The Dark Procession, Reviewed," 51 "Making a Sacher Torte," 56 "Joyce Carol Oates Plays the Saturn Piano," 61 "Why My Mother Likes Liberace."

(b) *Limited edition*:   1985

Title page, Collation, Pagination, & Contents as A66 a, save with extra leaves as noted below, and with colophon changed to read: "One hundred twenty-five hand numbered copies, signed by author and illustrator, of which fifty are *hors commerce*."

Binding: Bound in grey cloth over boards. Front: embossed publisher's emblem. White paper label pasted on spine, reading downward: [in black:] Diane Wakoski / [grey abstract design] / [in black:] Why My Mother Likes Liberace. This edition has two extra leaves bound in, both unprinted. The first is between pp. [12–13] of A66 a; the second follows p. [72] of A66 a.

Dust jacket: Issued in a clear acetate dust jacket.

Publication: Published by the SUN/gemini Press, Tucson, Arizona, in 1985 at $75.00. Edition size was 121 copies. 75 copies were for sale. 40 copies were numbered and marked "H.C." (*hors commerce*).

Note: According to DW, the book was not completed until January 1986.

B. Books Coauthored

B1   Four Young Lady Poets   1962

[in black:] FOUR YOUNG / LADY POETS / CAROL BERGÉ / BAR-BARA MORAFF / ROCHELLE OWENS / DIANE WAKOSKI / TOTEM PRESS / *in association with* / CORINTH BOOKS / 32 West Eighth Street / New York 11, New York

Collation: pp. [1-48]; 8″ × 5 1/4″; printed on wove paper.

Pagination: p. [1] title page, p. [2] copyright, pp. [3-4] NOTE ON THE AUTHORS, pp. [5-47] text, p. [48] list of Corinth paperbacks.

Binding: issued in white paper wrappers, stapled, with orange abstract design front and back. Front cover: in black: FOUR YOUNG / LADY POETS / CAROL BERGÉ / BARBARA MORAFF / ROCHELLE OWENS / DIANE WAKOSKI / TOTEM [slash] CORINTH $1.25.

Publication: Published by Totem/Corinth, New York, 1962, at $1.25. Edition size is unknown.

Contents: [36-41] "The Starving Vicuna," [42] "Journey," [43] "The Tightrope Walker," [43] "Cock Fight under the Magnolias," [44] "Black Leather, Because Bumble Bees Look Like It," [45-47] "My Chinese Fairy Tales for La Monte, who dislikes the obvious."

Note: LeRoi Jones was the uncredited editor of this publication. According to DW, the title of the book was intentionally ironic.

B2   Dream Sheet   1965

[in black:] DREAM SHEET / edited / by / Diane / Wakoski / [copyright symbol] 1965 [the title is also printed, as above, on the right side of the title page, reading upward]

Collation: Broadsheet; 22″ × 17″, folded once to 11″ × 8 1/2″; printed on wove paper.

Publication: Published by the Hard Ware Press, New York, in 1965.

Contents: "Black Bad Things."

B3   A Play and Two Poems   1968

(a) *First edition*:

[rule of leaf ornaments printed in green] / [at right of single green leaf ornament, in black:] The Well Wherein A Deer's Head Bleeds / *A play for Winter Solstice* / *by Robert Kelly* / [single green leaf ornament] "These Worlds Have Always Moved In Harmony" / *by Ron Loewinsohn* / [single green leaf ornament] Talking From Christmas Country / *by Diane Wakoski* / [single green leaf ornament] Black Sparrow Press / Los Angeles 1968 / [rule of leaf ornaments printed in green, as above]

Collation: pp. [1–24]; 6 3/16″ × 4 3/4″; printed on wove paper.

Pagination: pp. [1–2] blank, p. [3] title, p. [4] blank, p. [5] half-title, p. [6] blank, pp. [7–11] text, p. [12] blank, p. [13] half-title, p. [14] blank, pp. [15–16] text, p. [17] half-title, p. [18] blank, pp. [19–23] text, p. [24] colophon.

Binding: Issued in red paper wrappers; sewn with tie inside. Green paper label pasted on front cover: [in black, below rule of leaf ornaments:] A PLAY AND / TWO POEMS / [two rules of leaf ornaments] / [publisher's emblem] a christmas greeting from / the black sparrow press. Green endsheets tucked under flaps of wrappers. Issued in white mailing envelope.

Publication: Published by Black Sparrow Press, Los Angeles, 1 December 1968, and distributed gratis as a Christmas greeting from the Press. The colophon announces 400 copies, 100 of which comprise the variant binding described below. According to the publisher, "226 copies, 74 less than the announced limitation" of this issue were printed.

Contents: "Talking From Christmas Country."

(b) *Variant binding*:   1968

Title page, Collation, Pagination, & Contents as B3 a, except adds dark green flyleaves. 100 numbered and signed copies.

B4   The Wise Men Drawn to Kneel in Wonder   1971

(a) *First edition*:

[beneath violet circle ornament, in red:] David Bromige / THE NEST /
[double rule of violet circle ornaments, as above] / [in red:] Robert Kelly /
YESOD & MALKUTH, THAT IS, / ADVENT & CHRISTMAS. /
FROM "SPHERES" / [double rule of violet circle ornaments, as above] / [in
red:] Diane Wakoski / THE MAGI / [single violet circle ornament, as
above] / [in violet:] BLACK SPARROW PRESS / Los Angeles — 1971

Collation: pp. [1–16]; 5 5/8" × 4 1/8"; printed on wove paper.

Pagination: pp. [1–2] blank, p. [3] "A Christmas Greeting / from the / Black
Sparrow Press" / [publisher's emblem], p. [4] blank, p. [5] title page, p. [6]
copyright, pp. [7–12] text, pp. [13–14] blank, p. [15] publisher's note, p. [16]
blank.

Binding: Issued in light brown wrappers. Front: [rule of red circle ornaments]
/ [rule of blue circle ornaments] / [in red:] The wise men DRAWN / to kneel
in wonder at / the FACT so of ITSELF / [five rules of circle ornaments]. Purple flyleaves. Sewn with tie inside.

Publication: Published by the Black Sparrow Press, Los Angeles, 3 December
1971, in an edition of 525 copies, and distributed as a Christmas Greeting
from the Press.

Contents: "The Magi."

Note: The cover title is the original title of the Bromige poem.

(b) *Limited edition*:

Title page, Collation & Pagination as B4 a, but at 5 3/4" × 4 1/2".

Binding: Bound in half red cloth with light brown boards. Cover printed as
wrappered issue. Purple endsheets.

Dust jacket: Issued in a clear acetate dust jacket.

Publication: Published by the Black Sparrow Press; no priority. According to
the publisher, edition size was "111 copies signed by the three authors, of
which 100 copies were numbered 1–100; 1 copy each was marked 'Publisher's
Copy,' 'Printer's Copy,' ' Binder's Copy,' and 'File Copy'; 3 copies were

marked 'Author's Copy'; and 4 copies were numbered and marked 'Presentation Copy.'"

B5   Unicorn Postcard Series II   1972

Collation: Portfolio; 6 1/2" × 5"; banded (with title on band) group of eight postcards; printed on various papers.

Publication: Published by the Unicorn Press, Santa Barbara, California, in 1972. The size of the edition is unknown. The postcards were issued separately beginning in 1967.

Contents: "This Water Baby." (See A21.)

Note: The other postcards were by W.S. Merwin, Kenneth Rexroth, Apollinaire, Arthur Secunda, Langston Hughes, and Robert Bly, and with a card entitled "Vow (Peace post card)."

B6   Burning Deck Postcards: The First Ten   [1975]

Collation: Portfolio; ten postcards issued in a brown envelope, 10" × 7". See also A41.

Publication: Published by the Burning Deck Press, Providence, Rhode Island (1975?). Size of the edition is unknown.

Contents: "A Lover Disregards Names."

Note: The other postcards are by Willilam Bronk, James Camp, Tom Disch, George Hodgkins, Eli M. Mile, Keith Waldrop, Rosmarie Waldrop, Brick Washington, and Kirk Wilson.

B7   Burning Deck Postcards: The Second Ten   [1975]

Collation: Portfolio; 7" × 10"; ten postcards issued in an envelope. See also A41.

Publication: Published by the Burning Deck Press, Providence, Rhode Island, (1975?), in an edition of 100 copies.

Contents: "Claws."

Note: The other postcards are by James Camp, Nancy Condee, Tom Disch, Ray Ragosta, Carl Sesar, Mark Strand, John Taggart, Keith Waldrop, and Kirk Wilson.

B8   Burning Deck Postcards: The Third Ten   [1975]

Collation: Portfolio; 4 5/8″ × 7″; contains ten postcards. See also A41.

Publication: Published by the Burning Deck Press, Providence, Rhode Island, (1975?), at $2.50. 150 copies were printed.

Contents: "Comparisons."

Note: The other postcards are by Aliki Barnstone, Michael Benedikt, James Camp, Nancy Condee, E. Hope-McCarthy, Lissa McLaughlin, Eli M. Mile, Arthur Oberg, and Rosmarie Waldrop.

B9   The Last Poem [and] Tough Company   1976

(a) *First edition*:

[within brown rule frame, in red:] THE LAST POEM [in brown:] by / [in blue:] Diane Wakoski / [in brown:] & / [in red:] TOUGH COMPANY [in brown:] by / [in blue:] Charles Bukowski / [beneath brown rule frame, in brown:] BLACK SPARROW PRESS : SANTA BARBARA

Collation: pp. [1–12]; 7 3/4″ × 5″; printed on wove paper.

Pagination: p. [1] title page, p. [2] copyright, pp. [3–6] text of "The Last Poem," pp. [7–9] text of "Tough Company," p. [10] blank, p. [11] colophon: "Published January 1976/ as a New Year's Greeting / to the friends of the / Black Sparrow Press. / 176 copies of this edition / have been handbound / in boards and are / numbered and signed / by the authors," p. [12] blank.

Binding: Bound in stiff tan paper wrappers. Sewn with tie inside. Front cover: [within blue rule outer frame and orange rule inner frame, illustration in green of tree and birds] / [blue rule] / [within green inner rule frame, in red:] A NEW YEAR'S GREETING / *from the* / BLACK SPARROW PRESS / 1976. Blue flyleaves. Issued in a white paper mailing envelope. Designed by Barbara Martin.

Publication: Published by the Black Sparrow Press, Santa Barbara, California, 14 January 1976, for distribution gratis. Edition size was 740 copies.

Contents: "The Last Poem."

(b) *Hardcover edition*:   1976

Title page, Collation, & Pagination as B9 a.

Binding: Bound in half orange cloth with tan paper over boards, printed as wrappered issue. Blue flyleaves and endpapers.

Dust jacket: Issued in an unprinted white paper dust jacket.

Publication: Published by the Black Sparrow Press, Santa Barbara, California, 14 January 1976, for distribution gratis. Edition size was 150 numbered copies, signed by both authors.

(c) *Limited edition*:   1976

Title page, Collation, Pagination, & Binding as B9 b.

Dust jacket: Issued in an unprinted red paper dust jacket.

Publication: Published by the Black Sparrow Press, Santa Barbara, California, 14 January 1976, for distribution gratis. Edition size was 33 copies, signed by both authors. 26 copies were lettered A–Z. Two copies were marked "Author's Copy." One copy each was marked "Publisher's Copy," "Printer's Copy," "Binder's Copy," and "File Copy," and one copy was set aside as a presentation copy.

B10   The Feathery Tune   1980

Collation: Broadside; 17 3/4″ × 21 1/4″; prints three poems with caption titles.

Publication: Published by the "Sunset Canyon Recreation Center, UCLA campus, Wed. April 30th 1980." Edition size was 200 copies.

Contents: "The Feathery Tune" by DW, with "For aime Cesaire" by Clayton Eshleman and "At the Castle" by Jerome Rothenberg.

B11   Garvin's Poetry Show   1980

Collation: Xerox of holograph poem in white cardboard folder, 11 3/4″ × 9 1/2″. Fifteen leaves of 8 1/2″ × 11″ white paper, with the DW poem on the thirteenth.

Publication: Privately published in 1980.

Contents: "Adventures on a Balcony Overlooking the Morning Ocean."

B12   **Earth/Light**   1981

[in black:] earth [slash] light / DIANE WAKOSKI / KATHLEEN
SPIVACK / ELIZABETH MCKIM / MARGE PIERCY / GAIL MAZUR
/ MAXINE KUMIN / FANNY HOWE / RUTH WHITMAN / TESS
GALLAGHER / Pomegranate Editions 1981 /.

Collation: pp. [i–vi] 1-4 [4a-4b] 5-16 [17] 18-20 [20a-20b] 21-26 [27] 28
[29-30]; 10 1/[?]″ × 7 1/2″; printed on wove paper.

Pagination: pp. [i–ii] woodcut illustrations, p. [iii] title page, p. [iv] copyright
and acknowledgments, p. [v] preface by Kathleen Spivack, p. [vi] illustration, pp. 1-4 text, pp. [4a-4b] illustrations, pp. 5-16 text, p. [17] illustration,
pp. 18-20 text, pp. [20a-20b] illustrations, pp. 21-26 text, p. [27] illustration, p. 28 text, p. [29] illustration, p. [30] colophon: "This is an edition of
450 Copies / Numbers 1-50 are signed by the authors. / This book is set in
14 pt. Bembo by George Mc Coubrey / Titles are set by hand in 18 pt. Bembo
Italic. / Handprinted designed and illustrated by Karyl Klopp / on
Ticonderoga Titex. The 50 Special Copies are printed / on Rives
Heavyweight and bound by hand / with handprinted paper over boards. /
Issued June 1981 by Pomegranate Editions / This is copy No. _____.

Binding: Issued in stiff black paper wrappers over yellow paper. Pink paper
label pasted on front, in black: earth [slash] light / DIANE WAKOSKI /
KATHLEEN SPIVACK / ELIZABETH MCKIM / MARGE PIERCY /
GAIL MAZUR / MAXINE KUMIN / FANNY HOWE / RUTH WHIT-
MAN / TESS GALLAGHER / [at right, reading upward:] new poems by
contemporary women writers Pomegranate Editions 1981 /. There is a second label, of yellow paper with a black woodcut illustration, pasted over the
first label at bottom and right of center.

Publication: Published by Pomegranate Editions, Massachusetts, in June
1981.

Contents: 14 "Leaving Waterloo," 26 "Orphée."

Note: "Diane Wakoski's poems have been submitted with the reservation that
she feels 'women's anthologies create an unnecessary separation between
men and women'" (p. 16).

B13   **Two Poems**   1981

[half circle design of wreath with flower and, in green:] TWO / POEMS / [in grey:] Written and Copyright held / by Galway Kinnell and Diane Wakoski / with Barry Moser's wood engraving / and all else by Red Ozier Press / for our friends this joyous / New Year of 1981 / [design of leaves and flowers]

Collation: pp. [1–8]; 6″ × 4″; printed on wove paper.

Pagination: p. [1] title page, p. [2] acknowledgment, p. [3] text, p. [4] blank, pp. [5–7] text, p. [8] blank.

Binding: Issued in a green paper wrapper. Sewn with tie inside. Front, in dark green: TWO / POEMS. Tan flyleaves.

Publication: Published by the Red Ozier Press, Madison, Wisconsin, in 1981 for friends of the Press.

Contents: 3 "Daybreak," by Galway Kinnell, 5 "Gardenias," by DW.

C. Contributions to Periodicals

1958

C1   *Poems*: "Shadows at Stone Henge [sic]," "Translates: Stray Dragon, Nevertheless Blue," *Occident* Fall 1958: 24,42. Note: DW is "Manager." *Occident* was published by the Associated Students, U of California, Berkeley. The Fall 1957 issue lists DW as a member of the "Editorial Staff."

C2   *Poems*: "The Mask & Pear," "Sketch," "Justice Is Reason Enough," *Occident* Winter 1958: 12-13,34. Note: DW is the editor.

1959

C3   *Poem*: "Poem" ["To the young man who left the flowers / on my desk one April afternoon . . ."], *Coastlines* 12 (Spring 1959): 33. Note: According to DW, this was her "first real publication." "This was sent to an editor who didn't know me."

C4   *Poems*: "The Realization of Difference," "Love Poem," "If Madness Is Loving Too Much," *Occident* Spring 1959: 6-8. Note: DW is the assistant editor.

C5   *Poem*: "The Realization of Difference," *Galley Sail Review* 1.4 (Autumn 1959): 4-5.

C6   *Poems*: "Jazz Musician," "Dialogue," *Galley Sail Review* 2.1 (Winter 1959-1960): 29-31.

1960

C7   *Poem*: "This Is Unreal, Thank God," *Venture* 3.4 (Spring–Summer 1960): 20.

C8   *Poems*: "The Morning," "Overweight Poem," "Mea Culpa," "Danny Boyarin," "Mordecai," "Notes toward View of Cosmos," *Blacklist* 6 [1960]: 23–25.

1961

C9   *Poems*: "If Madness Is Loving Too Much," "A Lecture — after John Cage," "The Few Silver Scales," "There Was a Time," "And This Is the Way the World Ends: Never," "Dark Windows," "Love Poem," *Beatitude/east* 17 (February 1961): 4–9.

C10   *Poem*: "Coins and Coffins under My Bed," *Trobar* 3 (1961): 5–6.

C11   *Poem*: "A Lonely Woman Visits the Museum," *Galley Sail Review* 10 (Winter 1961–1962): 35.

1962

C12   *Poems*: "Diamond Story," "Mountain Road," "Short Story," *Chelsea* 12 (September 1962): 82–89.

C13   *Poem*: "Incident of Cherries and Peaches," *Nomad/New York* 10–11 (Autumn 1962): 83.

C14   *Poems*: "The Lily," "Scale," "A Poem for a Child Standing on the Beach," "Drum," *Seventh Street* Fall–Winter 1962: 35–38.

C15   *Poem*: "The Tightrope Walker," *Sparrow* 18 (November 1962): 3.

C16   *Poem*: "Incommunicado," *Genesis West* 1 (Winter 1962–1963): 180–181.

C17   *Poem*: "Poem to the Man on My Fire Escape," *Poems from the Floating World* 4 (1962): 33–34.

C18   *Poem*: "Six of Cups," *Trobar* 4 (1962): 6–8.

1963

C19   *Poems*: "The Thistle in the Fountain," "Apricot Poem," "Rock," "Heart without Head Is Free," "The Man Who Paints Mountains," *TISH* 17 (January 1963): 3–6.

C20 *Poem*: "The Oedipus Within," *TISH* 18 (February 1963): 9.

C21 *Poem*: "The First Day," *Outsider* 1.3 (Spring 1963): 54.

C22 *Poem*: "Journey," *Midwest* 5–6 (Spring 1963): 52–53.

C23 *Poems*: "Italian Women," "On the Prairie," *Poets at Le Métro* 4 (April 1963): 14.

C24 *Poem*: "A Poem for the Yam Festival," *Elizabeth* 6 (October 1963): 19.

C25 *Poems*: "Tendencies We Have Already Seen," "Midas," *Carlton Miscellany* 4.4 (Fall 1963): 38–40.

C26 *Poems*: "Water Subjects," "King of Pentacles: This Figure Has No Special Description," *SET* 2 (Winter 1963–1964): 36–48.

C27 *Poem*: "The Empress # 3," *Matter* 1963: 11.

C28 *Poem*: "How Everything Including Dreams Hinges on Definition," *Judson Review* 1 (1963): 51–52.

C29 *Poem*: "Loneliness," *Parallax* 6 (1963): [16–17].

1964

C30 *Column*: "Software Report," *Hardware Poets Occasional* 2 (March 1964): 6.

C31 *Column*: "Software Report," *Hardware Poets Occasional* 3 (June 1964): 6–8. Note: DW is an editor.

C32 *Poem*: "Answer," *Wild Dog* 10 (September 1964): 9.

C33 *Poems*: "Medieval Tapestry and Questions," "Scene IV, from The Tenuous Connection of Dreams," *Prairie Schooner* 38 (Fall 1964): 222–224.

C34 *Column*: "Software Report," *Hardware Poets Occasional* 4 (October 1964): 1. Note: DW is an editor.

C35 *Poem*: "George Washington and the Pearl Necklace," *Wild Dog* 11 (28 October 1964): 24–26.

C36   *Poem*: "Beyond all Sense of Time," *Poetry Review* [U of Tampa] 2 (1964): [3].

C37   *Poem*: "Belly Dancer," *Poetry Review* [U of Tampa] 3 (1964): [12].

C38   *Poem*: "George Washington; the Whole Man," *Pogamoggan* 1 (1964): 122–126.

C39   *Poem*: "The Piano," *Coyote's Journal* 1 (1964): 10.

C40   *Poems*: "George Washington & the Invention of Dynamite," "Letter to the West," *Occidental Review* 4.1 (1964?): 40–41.

1965

C41   *Poem*: "The Old Impossibilities," *Ante* 1.3 (Spring 1965): 44–45.

C42   *Poem*: "The Ice Eagle," *Some/Thing* 1.1 (Spring 1965): 26–28.

C43   *Poems*: "Portrait of a Lady," "Ixohoxi," "The Blooming Flower Fades," "Everything Boils Down to Diamonds," *Island* 3 (17 March 1965): 40–44.

C44   *Poem*: "City Museum, Split," *Wormwood Review* 17 (April 1965): 6–7.

C45   *Poem*: Untitled ["Pig / guards the / secret / of the ground. . ."], *TISH* 30 (June 1965): 4. Note: also published as "Pig."

C46   *Poems*: "Anger Poem upon the Gift of Rubies," "Overlay of Old Numbers," "3 of Swords," *Chelsea* 17 (August 1965): 78–83.

C47   *Poem*: "Monday thru Friday," *Magazine* 2 (October 1965): [20–21].

C48   *Poem*: "The Priestess # 1," *Software* 2 (November 1965): 2. Note: DW is co-editor.

C49   *Poem*: "Blue Monday," *Some/Thing* 1.2 (Winter 1965): 65–67.

C50   *Poem*: "Black Bad Things," *Dream Sheet* (1965): [2]. Note: DW is the editor.

C51   *Poem*: "From A Go to B, If You Can Find It," *Now Now* 1965: 11.

C52   *Poem*: "George Washington # 7: Dinner, the Classical & Romantic," *SUM* 4 (1965): [18–19].

C53   *Poems*: "The Magician," "Splendid Answers," *Poetry Review* [U of Tampa] 4 (1965): [14].

C54   *Poem*: "Money over the Water," *Poetry Review* [U of Tampa] 5 (1965): [33].

C55   *Poem*: "The Preistess [sic] Number One," *Brown Paper* 1 (1965): [21].

C56   *Poem*: "Discrepancies," *Mary Jane Quarterly* 2.1 (c. 1965): [9–13].

1966

C57   *Poem*: "The Acts of Devotion (Part III)," *Salted Feathers* 3.1 (January 1966): 22.

C58   *Poem*: "George Washington, The Father of My Country," *El Corno Emplumado* 17 (January 1966): 61–65. Published in Mexico City in English.

C59   *Poem*: "Serious Poem for Serious People," *Io* 2 (February 1966): 72–74.

C60   *Poems*: "Rain Trip," "The Pteradactyl" [sic], "The Night George Stanley Came to Me in a Dream," "Music Not for the Dance," *Things* 3 (Spring 1966): 16–21.

C61   *Poem*: "Sleep Incantation," *Beloit Poetry Journal* 3 (Spring 1966): 48–49.

C62   *Poems*: "The King: The Tombed Egyptian One," "The Cufflink Jade," *Art and Literature* 9 (Summer 1966): 78–80.

C63   *Poem*: "The Waterfall," *Potpourri* 7–8 (Summer 1966): 22.

C64   *Poem*: "Medicine Bag Song," *WIN* [New York Workshop in Non-violence] 2.15–16 (August 1966): 24–25.

C65   *Poem*: "Rescue Poem," *Riverrun* 1.1 (October 1966): 23–26.

C66   *Poem*: "The 8th Train to Shannon," *Island* 2 (November 1966): 26.

C67   *Poems*: "Black Uncle Sam & Poor Ofay Me," "How Can I Deal with My Problems, Kenyusha," *Io* 3 (Winter 1966-1967): 77-78.

C68   *Poem*: "The Day of the Autobiographical Frog," *Ante* 2.1 (Winter 1966): 27-32.

C69   *Poem*: "The House of the Heart," *Riverrun* 1.4 (1966): 4-6.

C70   *Poem*: "George Washington Dreams of Paratroop Forces," *Magazine* 3 (1966): 22-23.

C71   *Poem*: "Love Poem to the Magician," *Intrepid* 6 (1966): 49.

C72   *Poem*: "Speonk, Because It's a Favorite Word," *Vincent the Mad Brother of Theo* 1 (1966): 23. Note: The author's name is given as Diane Wakoski-Sherbell. DW appears in a cover photograph, pointing a gun at the camera.

C73   *Poems*: "Set: The Okapi," "Knots," "The Picture Frame Interest," *Out of Sight* 1.1 (1966): 19-24.

1967

C74   *Poem*: "Slicing Oranges for Joshua," *Haravec* 2 (March 1967): 61-64. Published in English in Peru.

C75   *Poem*: "Sometimes Even My Knees Smile," *Poetmeat* 13 (Spring 1967): 8.

C76   *Poems*: "Summer," "This Beautiful Black Marriage," *Athanor* 1.1 (Spring 1967): 12-16.

C77   *Poem*: "Screw, a Technical Love Poem," *Chelsea* 20-21 (May 1967): 16-17.

C78   *Poems*: "The Goblet," "Journies [sic] by Water," "Inside the Nest," *World* 4 (June 1967): 12-13.

C79   *Poem*: "The Singer," *Village Voice* 12.38 (July 1967): 14.

C80   *Poem*: "The Mechanic," *Issue* 1 (August 1967): [35].

C81   *Poem*: "The Helms Bakery Man," *Baker's Weekly* 4 September 1967: 21. Note: The poet's name is given as "Diana Wakoski."

C82   *Poem*: "Woman Holding the Skins of the Orchestra," *Weed* 11 (September –October 1967): 11.

C83   *Poem*: "Poet at the Carpenter's Bench," *El Corno Emplumado* 24 (October 1967): 86–88. Published in English in Mexico City.

C84   *Poem*: "The Ruby Necklace," *Analecta* 1 (Fall 1967): 6–7.

C85   *Review*: Rev. of *The Making of the Christian West*, by Georges Duby, and *The Portrait in the Renaissance*, by John Pope-Hennessy, *Arts Magazine* 9 (1967): n. pag.

C86   *Poem*: "Sky," *Target* 4 (1967): 2–3. Published in England. Note: The poet's name is given as Diane Wakoski-Sherbell.

1968

C87   *Poem*: "To My Friends Who Talk about the Revolution," *Noose* 1 (23 March 1968): [7–8].

C88   *Poem*: "The Universes," *The LIT* 7 (May 1968): 17–22.

C89   *Poem*: "The Best Gun & the Lace Cuff," *Northwest Review* 10.1 (Summer 1968): 56–63.

C90   *Poems*: "Instructions for Growing Laburnam on the Buddha's Birthday," "Poem for a Man Who Is Sleeping on the Buddha's Birthday," "A Message to Someone I Love on the Buddha's Birthday," *Noose* 7 (27 July 1968): [3].

C91   *Poems*: "Stepping to the Dream Letter Box in Her Mother-of-Pearl Shoes," "The Silver Psych-Out," "The Eyes of Death Watering on the Desert," *Sou'wester* 2.2 (Fall 1968): 11–15.

C92   *Poems*: "The Buddha Has His Birthday in Court," "George Washington Sends a Pair of Shoebuckles to the Buddha on His Birthday," "The Elephant & the Butterfly Meet on the Buddha's Birthday," *Denver Quarterly* 3.3 (Autumn 1968): 92–94.

C93   *Poems*: "A Long Poem for Eleanor Who Collects the Blood of Poets," "That Delicate Displacement of Reality on the Buddha's Birthday," "The Blue World Holds the Sun as a Rake on Buddha's Birthday," *Bones* 2 (Winter 1968–1969): 44–50.

C94	*Poems*: "Buddha's Birthday," "Buddha Has His Birthday in Court," "A Long Trainride without a Calendar Showing Buddha's Birthday," "Letter to Carol Bergé on Buddha's Birthday," *Odda Tala* 1 (1968): [3–6].

C95	*Poem*: "The House of My Heart," *I-Kon: Five Artists, Five Poets* 1968: n. pag.

C96	*Poems*: "Instructions for Growing Laburnam on the Buddha's Birthday," "The Buddha Runs a Race on His Birthday," "Bank Statement on the Buddha's Birthday," "The Buddha Learns to Work a Radial Arm Saw on His Birthday," "A Message to Someone I Love on the Buddha's Birthday," "George Washington Sends a Pair of Shoebuckles to the Buddha on His Birthday," "Poem for a Man Who Is Sleeping on the Buddha's Birthday," "Poem for a Little Boy on the Buddha's Birthday," "Judge Not, Says the Buddha on His Birthday," *Odda Tala* 2 (1968): [1–9].

C97	*Poems*: "The Night a Sailor Came to Me in a Dream," "Summer," "Sun," "The Empress," *Minnesota Review* 8.2 (1968): 138–140.

C98	*Poem*: "Ringless," *Penumbra* 1.3–4 (1968): 31–33.

1969

C99	*Poem*: "Love Passes beyond the Incredible Hawk of Innocence," *Caterpillar* 2.1, no. 6 (January 1969): 98–103.

C100	*Poem*: "Greed: Part IV Intruders," *Noose* 12 (8 February 1969): [2–6].

C101	*Poem*: "Indian Giver," *Noose* 13 (8 March 1969): [4].

C102	*Poem*: "An Hour," *Caterpillar* 2.2, no. 7 (April 1969): 65–69.

C103	*Poems*: "Love Letter Postmarked Von Beethoven [sic]," "My Trouble," "Being a Landlord of the Emotions," *Sumac* 1.3 (Spring 1969): 34–38.

C104	*Poem*: "The Moon Cock Waking Me after Dreaming of Foxes," *Occident* ns 3 (Spring–Summer 1969): 70–71.

C105	*Poems*: "Love Letter Postmarked Von Beethoven [sic]," "An Anti-War Poem," "The Man in the Mirror/Moon," "A Bank Statement on the

Buddha's Birthday," "The Delicate Displacement of Reality on the Buddha's Birthday," "Instructions for Growing Laburnam on the Buddha's Birthday," *Poetry Bag* 2.3 (Summer 1969): 9–15.

C106 *Poems*: "A Poet Recognizing the Echo of the Voice," "The Lament of the Lady Bank Dick," *Caterpillar* 2.3–4, nos. 8–9 (July–October 1969): 119–126.

C107 *Poem*: "Caves," *Concerning Poetry* 2.2 (Fall 1969): 29–31.

C108 *Poem*: "A Little Poem for the Calligrapher on the Buddha's Birthday," *Bricoleur* 1 (September 1969): [31–32].

C109 *Poem*: "The Birds of Paradise Being Very Plain Birds," *The Sage* 12 (October 1969): 20–22.

C110 *Poems*: "My Hell's Angel," selections from "Sister Diane's Book of the Zodiac," *Noose* 19 (25 October 1969): [11–15].

C111 *Poems*: "Reaching Out with the Hands of the Sun," "Thanking My Mother for Piano Lessons," *The Ant's Forefoot* 3 (Winter 1969): 2–5.

C112 *Poem*: "No More Soft Talk," *New American Review* 7 (1969): 169–171.

C113 *Poems*: Selections from *The Moon Has a Complicated Geography*. *Odda Tala* 3 (1969): [5–18]. Note: The entire issue is devoted to DW's poems.

C114 *Poems*: "Sunflowers in My Wrist," "I Lay Next to You All Night, Trying Awake to Understand the Watering Places of the Moon," *Stony Brook* 3–4 (1969): 77–79.

C115 *Poem*: "The Universes," *Mad Windows* 1969: 5–10.

C116 *Poems*: "Past Another Life," "Page of Cups," "Fire," "Pig," *Mother* 12 [1969?]: 5.

1970

C117 *Poem*: "The Ten Dollar Cab Ride," *Lillabulero* 8 (Winter 1970): 60–63.

C118 *Poem*: "Film: Called 5 Blind Men," *Sumac* 2.2–3 (Winter–Spring 1970): 70–77.

C119   *Poem*: "The Night a Sailor Came to Me in a Dream," *The Georgian* 33.23 (21 January 1970): 3.

C120   *Poem*: "My Aunt Ella Meets the Buddha on His Birthday," *Antioch Review* 30.1 (Spring 1970): 34–36.

C121   *Poem*: "Exorcism," *Shaded Room* 1 (March 1970): 19.

C122   *Poem*: "In Place of a Phone Call to Arabia," *The Nation* 210.10 (16 March 1970): 317.

C123   *Poem*: "I Have Had to Learn to Live with My Face," *Caterpillar* 3.2, no. 10 (April 1970): 78–81.

C124   *Essay*: "What the Poet Needs from Society," *New York Quarterly* (program for *New York, New York* at Circle in the Square Theatre, New York, 25 May 1970): 6–7.

C125   *Poem*: "Call Me Ishmael," *Pulse* 3 (Summer 1970): [18].

C126   *Poems*: "Winter Ode," "For a (1) Cold, (2) Hard, (3) Mean, (4) Nasty, (5) None of These, Sculptor I Like," *Tuatera* 2 (June 1970): 13–17.

C127   *Poem*: "The Night Rides of My Neighbor Lorca, That Prevent Sleep," *Lillabulero* 9 (Summer–Fall 1970): 47–49.

C128   *Poems*: "The Ten Dollar Cab Ride," "In Place of a Phone Call to Arabia," "Fire Message," *Desert Review* Summer–Autumn 1970: 1–5.

C129   *Poem*: "Five Love Poems," *Kayak* 21 (1970): 12.

C130   *Poem*: "Glass," *Choice* 6 (1970): 19–23.

C131   *Poem*: "A Poem for My 32nd Birthday," *Friendly Local Press* 1.6 (1970): 6–10.

C132   *Poem*: "Quicksilver Sailor's Daughter," *OPUS* 7 (1970): 53.

C133   *Poems*: "Uneasy Rider," "My Hell's Angel," *Hearse* 12 (1970): 1–7.

C134   *Poems*: "Exorcism," "Wishbones," *Hearse* 13 (1970): 2–5.

1971

C135   *Poems*: "The Catalogue of Charms," "Quicksilver Sailor's Daughter," *Lemming* 1 (Winter 1971): 29–31.

C136   *Poem*: "Thanking My Mother for Piano Lessons," *Mediterranean Review* 1.2 (Winter 1971): 72–76.

C137   *Poem*: "To an Autocrat," *Caterpillar* 4.2, no. 14 (January 1971): 123–125.

C138   *Poem*: "Smudging," *Poetry* 117.6 (March 1971): 351–355.

C139   *Poems*: "Some Talking Blues," "Love Is Just an Old Buick," *Tuatara* 4 (March 1971): 4–8.

C140   *Poem*: "Anticipation of Sharks," *Armadillo* 1 (Spring 1971): 15.

C141   *Poems*: "With Words," "The Mechanic," "The Desert Motorcyclist," "Uneasy Rider," "Letter to Shep, Letter Number One," "Letter Number Two — Airplane Letter," "Letter Number Three," "You, Letting the Trees Stand as My Betrayer," *The Falcon* 2–3 (Spring 1971): 26–42. Note: This issue also contains an interview by W.A. Blais, "The Poet Places Herself: An Interview with Diane Wakoski."

C142   *Poems*: "Placing a $2 Bet for a Man Who Will Never Go to the Horse Races Any More," "Conversations with Jan," "Sunpoem," *Crazy Horse* 7 (June 1971): 15–17.

C143   *Poem*: "My Knees Go before the Firing Squad at Sunrise," [with an editor's note on the poem and DW's reply to the note] *Works* 3.1 (Summer–Fall 1971): 30–34.

C144   *Poem*: "To the Wives," *Mediterranean Review* 2.1 (Fall 1971): 69–71.

C145   *Review*: "Songs & Notes," *Poetry* 118.6 (September 1971): 355–358. Reviews *Songs*, by Robert Kelly, and *Somewhere Among Us a Stone Is Taking Notes*, by Charles Simic.

C146   *Poem*: "The Joyful Black Demon of Sister Clara Flies through the Midnight Woods on Her Snowmobile," *Caterpillar* 5.1, no. 17 (October 1971): 90–98.

C147   *Poem*: "The Marshall," *Unmuzzled Ox* 1.1. (November 1971): 13.

C148   *Review*: "Working Poet," *N. Y. Review of Books* 30 December 1971:
26. Review of *Poems 1934–1969*, by David Ignatow.

C149   *Poem*: "Wishbones," *Rainbow Snake* 1 [San Diego State College]
(1971): 32–33.

1972

C150   *Poems*: "I Have Had to Learn to Live With My Face," "Thanking
My Mother for Piano Lessons," *Cosmopolitan* 172.2 (February 1972): 104+ .

C151   *Poem*: Untitled ["In Texas / no woman wears a size 32 brassiere"],
Out of Sight 43 (February 1972): [7].

C152   *Poems*: Selections from *Smudging*. *Unmuzzled Ox* 1.2 (February
1972): 46–52.

C153   *Poem*: "Magicians," *The Falcon* 4 (Spring 1972): 30–32.

C154   *Poem*: "V. The Green Bird," *Lampeter Muse* 7.1 (Spring 1972):
35–36.

C155   *Poem*: "What I Want in a Husband besides a Mustache,"
Cosmopolitan 172.4 (April 1972): 108.

C156   *Poems*: "When Black Is a Color Because It Follows a Grey Day,"
"Those Trigger Fish Again," *Ikon* 1 (May 1972): 25–26.

C157   *Poem*: "Transformations," *Open Reading* 2 (Fall 1972): 2–3.

C158   *Poems*: "Gold," "Some Constantly Besieged Castle," *Poetry
Miscellany* 2.1 (Fall–Winter 1972–1973): 22–25.

C159   *Reviews*: "20th Century Music," "A Satirist in the Avant-Garde,"
Parnassus: Poetry in Review 1.1. (Fall–Winter 1972): 142–151. Reviews of *Poems
for the Game of Silence*, by Jerome Rothenberg, and *The Tables I–XV*, by Armand Schwerner.

C160   *Poem*: "Love Letter Postmarked Van Beethoven," *Cosmopolitan*
173.4 (October 1972): 217.

C161   *Poems*: "What the Struggle Is All About," "I Am the Daughter of
the Sun," "Offering to Trade Lives with the Clam," *Cimarron Review* 21 (October 1972): 6–9.

C162   *Poem*: "The Skier," *Cavalier Daily* [U of Virginia] 3 November 1972, Supplement: 2.

C163   *Poem*: "Beyond the Wall Covered with Morning Glories," *The Nation* 215.15 (13 November 1972): 476.

C164   *Column*: "The Craft of Plumbers, Carpenters, & Mechanics," *American Poetry Review* 1.1. (November –December 1972): 46–47.

C165   *Poem*: "Belly Dancer," *Dance Perspectives* 52 (Winter 1972): 38.

C166   *Poem*: "The Mirror of a Day Chiming Marigolds," *Amaranthus* 7 (Winter 1972): 33–35.

C167   *Poem*: "Those Mythical Silver Pears," *Tens* 4 (December 1972): 5.

C168   *Letter*: Untitled, *Cavalier Daily* [U of Virginia] 8 December 1972, Supplement: 6.

C169   *Essay*: "Form Is an Extension of Content," *Sparrow* 3 (15 December 1972): [1–13]. Rpt. in *Sparrow 1–12*. Los Angeles: Black Sparrow Press, 1973.

C170   *Poem*: "To a Friend Who Cannot Accept My Judgment of Him," *Equal Time* 1972: 91–93.

C171   *Poem*: "Transformations," *Kayak* 28 (1972): 28–29.

C172   *Poems*: "Water," "The Cool Star," *Gegenschein Quarterly* 1.4 (1972): [7–8].

C173   *Poem*: "Wednesday," *Magazine* 5 (1972): 10–11.

C174   *Poems*: "When the Shoe Fits," "Her Throat," "Poem Dressed in a White Baggy Suit," *Ironwood* 1 (1972): 38–40.

1973

C175   *Column*: "A Tribute to Anaïs Nin," *American Poetry Review* 2.1 (January–February 1973): 46–47.

C176   *Column*: "Form Is an Extension of Content: Second Lecture," *American Poetry Review* 2.2 (March–April 1973): 18–19.

C177   *Column*: "The Emerald Essay," *American Poetry Review* 2.3
(May–June 1973): 15–16.

C178   *Review*: Rev. of *Altars*, by Clayton Eshleman, and *Threads*, by
David Bromige, *Vort* 3 (Summer 1973): 40–42.

C179   *Poems*: "Those Mythical Pears," "Some Brilliant Sky," "I Take the
Green Greed onto the Freeway," *Works* 4.1 (Summer 1973): 4–7.

C180   *Poem*: "The Story of Richard Maxfield," *Poetry* 122.4 (July 1973):
206–208.

C181   *Poem*: "Memories of Meeting Michael," *Chelsea* 32 (August 1973):
45–47.

C182   *Column*: "The Craft of Plumbers, Carpenters, & Mechanics,"
American Poetry Review 2.4 (August–September 1973): 17–18.

C183   *Column*: "The Craft of Plumbers, Carpenters, & Mechanics,"
American Poetry Review 2.5 (September–October 1973): 55–56.

C184   *Poem*: "When Black Is a Color Because It Follows a Grey Day,"
Ms. October 1973: 77.

C185   *Column*: "The Craft of Plumbers, Carpenters, & Mechanics,"
American Poetry Review 2.6 (November–December 1973): 20 + .

C186   *Poem*: "The Dream, All Her Pale Blue Leather Books," *Inlet* 2
(1973): 35–36.

C187   *Poem*: "Trying to Read by the Light of Shooting Stars," *Cotton* [U
of Alabama] 1.1 (1973): 5.

1974

C188   *Column*: "The Craft of Plumbers, Carpenters, & Mechanics,"
American Poetry Review 3.1 (January–February 1974): 46–47.

C189   *Poem*: "To Harry Lewis Who Said, 'Art cannot ask for in-
dulgence. It must in fact be an attack on that very thing,'" *Scholastic* 115.10
(1 March 1974): 22. Note: This issue of *Scholastic* also comprises the first
number of the *Notre Dame Review*.

C190   *Column*: "The Craft of Plumbers, Carpenters, & Mechanics," *American Poetry Review* 3.2 (March–April 1974): 36–38.

C191   *Poems*: "Dear Michael," "Whistling," "Telling You True about My Fantasy Life," "Discovering Michael as the King of Spain," "Touching the King of Spain under Water," "In Praise of Modern Times," *Sparrow* 21 (18 June 1974): [1–13]. Note: The entire issue is given to these poems. Rpt. in *Sparrow 13–24*. Los Angeles: Black Sparrow Press, 1974.

C192   *Poems*: "Walking past Paul Blackburn's Apt. on 7th St.," "A Poem with a Blackburn Beginning," *Lakes & Prairies* 1.1 (Fall 1974): 37–39.

C193   *Poem*: Untitled ["Returning to the Euycalyptus of my childhood..."], *Mosaic* 6 (Fall 1974): 16.

C194   *Poem*: "Lemon, Garlic, & Pepper," *Mosaic* 7 (Winter 1974): 22–23.

C195   *Poems*: "Poem Beginning with a Line from a Zebra," "Blessing Ode for a Man with Fish Bones around His Neck," "Lips, Opening," "Stillife: Michael, Silver Flute and Violets," *Poetry Review* 65.1 (1974): 18–25. Published in England.

C196   *Poem*: "Stillife: Michael, Silver Flute and Violets," *Mundus Artium* 7.2 (1974): 68–69.

1975

C197   *Poem*: "Recognizing that My Wrists Always Have Salmon Leaping for Spring in Them," *Hecate* 1.1 (January 1975): 48–49.

C198   *Poem*: "Bracelets," *Paintbrush* 3 (Spring 1975): 14.

C199   *Poem*: "A Winter Poem for Tony Weinburger Written on the Occasion of Feeling Very Happy," *Trellis* 2 (Spring 1975): 24–25.

C200   *Essay*: "Creating a Personal Mythology," *Sparrow* 31 (28 April 1975): [1–12]. Rpt. in *Sparrow 25–36*. Los Angeles: Black Sparrow Press, 1975.

C201   *Poems*: From "Fifteen Poems for a Lunar Eclipse None of Us Saw," *Greenhouse Review* 1 (Summer 1975): 8–14. Note: Includes parts I, III, IV, VI, X, XIV, and XV.

C202   *Poem*: "Harry Moon from My Child's Anthology of Verse," *Grove* 1 (Summer 1975): 16–21.

C203   *Poem*: "How Do You Tell a Story?," *Hecate* 1.2 (July 1975): 57–60.

C204   *Poem*: "A Drab Beach Reminds Me of a Crippled Woman," *Review '75* 2 (September 1975): 49.

C205   *Poems*: "Beyond the Trunks of the Palm Trees," "Precisely, Not Violets," "April Snow," "A Shipment of George Washington Apples Arrives in a Snowstorm," "Looking for the King of Spain," *Boundary* 2 (Fall 1975): 202–209.

C206   *Essay*: "Diane Wakoski on Little Magazines and Their Editors," *Gravida* 5 (Winter 1975): 26–29.

C207   *Poems*: "Counting Your Blessings on All Six Fingers of Your Hand: A Vigil," "Life Is Like a Game of Cards, or Another One of Those Metaphysical Statements from a Dated Reader," "Poem Beginning with a Line from a Zebra," "To the Young Man Who Left Flowers on My Desk One April Afternoon," *Poetry Now* 2.3 (1975): 8–10.

C208   *Poem*: "Five Love Poems," *Kayak* 21 (1975): 12.

C209   *Essay*: "The True Art of Simplicity: An Appreciation of George Oppen," *Ironwood* 5 (1975): 31–34.

1976

C210   *Review*: "A Woman Speaks," *N.Y. Times Book Review* 81.1 (4 January 1976): 3–4. Review of *The Lectures, Seminars, and Interviews of Anaïs Nin*, ed. Evelyn J. Hinz.

C211   *Poem*: "George Washington Meets the King of Spain (on the Magellanic Clouds)," *Red Cedar Review* 10.2–3 (May 1976): 103.

C212   *Essay*: "Variations on a Theme (An Essay on Revision)," *Sparrow* 50 (1 November 1976): [1–16]. Rpt. in *Sparrow 49–60*. Santa Barbara, California: Black Sparrow Press, 1977.

C213   *Poem*: "Tearing Up My Mother's Letters," *Faire* [Whitman College] 3.1 (November 1976): 26–28.

C214   *Poem*: "To the Lion," *The Poet's Image: The Photographer's Eye* [exhibit catalog, Long Island U] 1976: [30].

1977

C215   *Poem*: "Running Men," *Cornell Review* 1 (Spring 1977): 81–83.

C216   *Poem*: "Overnight Projects with Wood," *Red Cedar Review* 11.2 (May 1977): 5–6.

C217   *Poems*: "The Ring," "Tearing Up My Mother's Letters," "The Hitchhikers," *Poetry* 130.3 (June 1977): 125–130.

C218   *Poems*: "George Washington Sends a Pair of Shoebuckles to the Buddha on His Birthday," "The Delicate Displacement of Reality on Buddha's Birthday," "The Buddha Runs a Race on His Birthday," "The Dream of Angling, the Dream of Cool Rain," "For Whitman," *AURA* 7 (Fall 1977): 85–89.

C219   *Poems*: "A Poem in Response to Rexroth, Irish Coffee, a Day Alone, Forgiving Men, for They Have No Wombs, No Treasury, No Sense of the Infinite Possession of Self," "Life Is Like a Game of Cards, or Another One of Those Metaphysical Statements from a Distant Reader," *Centennial Review* 21.4 (Fall 1977): 382–387.

C220   *Essay*: "The Blue Swan, an Essay on Music in Poetry," *A Shout in the Street* 1.3 (1977): 23–35.

C221   *Poem*: "To the Thin and Elegant Woman Who Resides inside of Alix Nelson," *Gravida* 12 (1977): 8–11.

1978

C222   *Poem*: "Searching for the Canto Fermo," *Missouri Review* 1.1 (Spring 1978): 30.

C223   *Poem*: "Pachelbel's Canon," *Sparrow* 71 (9 August 1978): entire issue. Rpt. in *Sparrow 61–72*. Santa Barbara, California: Black Sparrow Press, 1978.

1979

C224   *Poems*: "On the Subject of Roses," "Bracelets," *Southern Review* 15.1 (Winter 1979): 138–139.

C225   *Poems*: "Measuring," "For a Man Who Learned to Swim When He Was Sixty," *New Letters* 45.3 (Spring 1979): 55–57.

C226   *Poem*: "Pamela's Green Tomato Pie," *Atlantic Review* ns 1 (Spring 1979): 26–27.

C227   *Poem*: "Calla Lily," *Missouri Review* 3.1 (Autumn 1979): 13.

C228   *Poem*: "My Mother's Milkman," *Louisville Review* 7 (Fall 1979): 17–19.

C229   *Poem*: "Nell's Birthday," *Plainsong* 1.2 (Fall 1979): 34–35.

C230   *Essay*: "Paradox," *Voices* 15.3 (Fall 1979): 58–60. Note: Following the essay are comments by Vin Rosenthal, Hedi McKinley, James E. Dublin, and Virginia Fraser Stern (60–62).

C231   *Poems*: "Red Runner," "Red Runner Again," *Cornell Review* 7 (Autumn 1979): 93–94.

1980

C232   *Poems*: "The Cap of Darkness," "Aging," "Silver," "Precision," "White," *Cedar Rock* 5.1 (Winter 1980): 6–7.

C233   *Poem*: "Green Thumb," *Iowa Review* 11.2–3 (Spring–Summer 1980): 94–98.

C234   *Poem*: "Sailor's Daughter," *Apropos* 1.6 (August–September 1980): 11. Note: A profile of DW is also printed.

C235   *Poem*: "Breakfast," *Southern Poetry Review* 20.2 (Autumn 1980): 5–6.

C236   *Review*: "The Poet as Prophet," *American Book Review* 2.6 (September –October 1980): 15. A review of *The Bus to Veracruz*, by Richard Shelton.

C237   *Poem*: "Stillife: Michael, Silver Flute, and Violets," *Mundus Artium* 12–13 (1980–1981): 332–333.

C238   *Poem*: "Frog Mozart," *Stone Country* 7.3 (1980): 43–45.

C239   *Poem*: "Memory," *Corona* 1 (1980): 11.

C240   *Poem*: "My Mother's Milkman," *Tendril* 9 (1980): 163.

1981

C241   *Poem*: "The Dark Procession," *Cumberland Poetry Review* 1.1 (Winter 1981): 31–33. Note: The poet's name is given as "Diane Wakowski."

C242   *Poems*: "Sailor's Daughter," "Peaches," *Prairie Schooner* 55.1–2 (Spring–Summer 1981): 120–121.

C243   *Poem*: "For Clint on the Desert," *Tendril* 11 (Summer 1981): 78–79.

C244   *Poem*: "The Rose," *Southern Poetry Review* 21.2 (Autumn 1981): 65–66.

C245   *Poem*: "Morning Thunderstorm," *Connecticut Poetry Review* 1.1 (Winter 1981–1982): 26–27.

C246   *Article*: in "Responses to Frederick Turner," *Missouri Review* 5.2 (Winter 1981–1982): 171–197.

C247   *Poem*: "Nell's Birthday," *Three Rivers Poetry Journal* 17–18 (1981): 84–85.

C248   *Poem*: "Little Tricks of Linear B," *Ploughshares* 7.2 (1981): 72–79.

C249   *Poem*: "Why I Am a Poet Not a Painter," *Sulfur* 1 (1981): 195–198.

1982

C250   *Poems*: "Human History: Its Documents," "Paleolithic," *Cedar Rock* 7.1 (Winter 1982): 8.

C251   *Poems*: "A Letter to Weng Wei on the Season of Tumultuous Magicians," "Un Morceau en Forme de Poire," "Sally Plum," "Saturday Night," *Centennial Review* 26.1 (Winter 1982): 51–60.

C252   *Poem*: "Molokai," *Memphis State Review* 2.2 (Spring 1982): 48–51.

C253   *Essay*: "The Epigramatic [sic] Verse of Josephine Miles," *Epoch* 31.1 (Fall–Winter 1982): 77–81.

C254   *Poem*: "Whole Sum," *Green River Review* 13.1–2 (1982): 179–180.

1983

C255   *Poem*: "Sleeping in the Ring of Fire," *Tendril* 14–15 (Winter 1983): 209–210.

C256   *Review*: Rev. of *Nigredo: Selected Poems 1970–1980*, by Norman Weinstein, *Sulfur* 6 (1983): 168–171.

C257   *Review*: Rev. of *Passages toward the Dark*, by Thomas McGrath, *American Book Review* 5.4 (May–June 1983): 18.

C258   *Poems*: "For the Girl with Her Face in a Rose," "Joyce Carol Oates Plays the Saturn Piano," "The Ring of Irony," *Sulfur* 7 (1983): 27–35.

C259   *Review*: Rev. of *The Clouds of That Country* and *Selected Poems*, by Jack Anderson, *American Book Review* 5.6 (September–October 1983): 16.

C260   *Essay*: "Uneasy Rider," *American Poetry* 1.1 (Fall 1983): 77–80. Note: The essay appears as part of a forum. The other contributors are Shirley Kaufman, Denise Levertov, and Ruth Stone, and the forum is titled "Sexual Politics: Notes on Genre and Gender in Poetry by Women."

C261   *Review*: Rev. of *My Life*, by Lyn Hejinian, *Sulfur* 8 (1983): 205–208.

C262   *Poem*: "Personal & Impersonal Landscapes," *Little Balkans Review* 4.2 (Winter 1983–1984): 19–20.

1984

C263   *Review*: "Middle Class Poetry," *American Book Review* 6.2 (January–February 1984): 4–5. Reviews *The Objects in the Garden*, by Thomas Luhrmann, *Yellow Light*, by Garrett Kaoru Hongo, and *Presence*, by Alan Williamson.

C264   *Essay*: "Neglected Poets 1: The Attempt to Break an Old Mold—Visionary Poetry of Clayton Eshleman," *American Poetry* 1.3 (Spring 1984): 38–46. Note: Clayton Eshleman responds to this essay in *American Poetry* 2.2 (Winter 1985): 79–82.

C265   *Review*: "The Life of Albert Goldbarth?", *American Book Review* 6.4 (May–June 1984): 8. Review of *Original Light: New and Selected Poems 1973–1983*, by Albert Goldbarth.

C266   *Essay*: "Neglected Poets 2: William Everson and Bad Taste," *American Poetry* 2.1 (Fall 1984): 36–43.

C267   *Poem*: "10° of Leo," *Kentucky Poetry Review* 20.2 (Fall 1984): 127–128.

C268   *Essay*: "William Carlos Williams: The Poet's Poet," *Sagetrieb* 3.2 (Fall 1984): [43]–47.

C269   *Poems*: "Winning and Losing," "Gourds," "Head Life," "Amaryllis Belladonna," *Prairie Schooner* 58.4 (Winter 1984): 75–80.

C270   *Poem*: "Crocus," *Sierra Madre Review* 1.1 (Winter 1984–1985): 90–91.

C271   *Poems*: "When It Looks Like Rain," "Oxtail Stew," *Manhattan Poetry Review* 4 (Winter 1984–1985): 20–21.

C272   *Poems*: "The Doctor in His Car," "Making a Pressed Flower Book," "The Blue Jay," "The Ukrainian Rose," *Pacific Review* 2 (1984): 67–71.

C273   *Poem*: "The Orange," *Agni Review* 20 (1984): 72–73.

C274   *Poem*: "The Story of Richard Maxfield," *Pebble Magazine* 23 (1984): 32–35. Note: This is a special issue with the title *Poems for the Dead*.

1985

C275   *Poem*: "The Fear of Fat Children," *Denver Quarterly* 19.4 (Spring 1985): 37–39.

C276   *Poem*: "Why My Mother Likes Liberace," *Kentucky Poetry Review* 21.1 (Spring–Summer 1985): 30–31.

C277   *Poems*: "On Saturn, After M," "Collecting Rare Books/Haunting Junk Shops," "Something Which," *Manhattan Poetry Review* 5 (Summer–Fall 1985): 8–9.

C278   *Review*: "The Adult Wilhelmina," *American Book Review* 7.5 (July–August 1985): 12–13. Review of *Outsiders*, by Karen Snow.

C279   *Essay*: "The New American Poetry," *Poetry Flash* 150 (September 1985): 1+ .

C280   *Review*: "The Feminine Lurking at the Heart of Macho Poetry," *American Book Review* 7.6 (September–October 1985): 16–18. Reviews *Winter Eel*, by Norman Hindley, *Fishing the Backwash*, by Jack Driscoll, and *In a U-Haul North of Damascus*, by David Bottoms.

C281   *Poem*: "Earth," *Transfer* 50 (Fall 1985): 52–53.

C282   *Review*: Rev. of *Kenneth Patchen and American Mysticism*, by Ray Nelson, *Centennial Review* 24.4 (Fall 1985): 482–484.

C283   *Poems*: "On the Boardwalk in Atlantic City," "Braised Leeks & Framboise," *Virginia Quarterly Review* 61.4 (Autumn 1985): 625–628.

C284   *Essay*: "Neglected Poets 3: Robert Peters," *American Poetry* 2.2 (Winter 1985): 71–78.

C285   *Poems*: "New Slate," "Violets," *Blow* 7 (1985): [3–4].

C286   *Poem*: "Removed from Natural Habitat," *Burning World* 1 (1985): 6.

C287   *Poem*: "Reading the Pharmacist's Daughter's Letters," *Raccoon* 17 (1985): 11.

C288   *Poems*: "The Tree," "In Response to Grey," *Blow* 8 (1985): 4+ .

D. Contributions to Anthologies

D1 *Seventh Street: Poems from Les Deux Megots*. Don Katzman, ed. New York: Argentina Press, 1961. *Contains*: "Iris and the Broken Mirror," "Largely Because of Coincidence and Partly Because of Chance, I Have Taken Up a New Address at 47th Street and Avenue F."

D2 *A Controversy of Poets*. Paris Leary and Robert Kelly, eds. New York: Anchor-Doubleday, 1965. *Contains*: "Justice Is Reason Enough," "Poem to the Man on My Fire Escape," "Coins and Coffins under My Bed," "Apparitions Are Not Singular Occurrences," "Six of Cups," "The Empress." Note: DW also contributed an autobiographical statement which appears on p. 553.

D3 *Another Way Out*. Lois A. Michel, ed. New York: Holt, 1968. *Contains*: "The Priestess No. 1."

D4 *The Eastside Scene*. Allen DeLoach, ed. Buffalo: State U of New York at Buffalo UP, 1968. *Contains*: "The Birds of Paradise Being Very Plain Birds." Note: Republished by Anchor-Doubleday, New York, in 1972.

D5 *Technicians of the Sacred*. Jerome Rothenberg, ed. New York: Doubleday, 1968. *Contains*: "Blue Monday." Note: Republished by Anchor-Doubleday, New York, in 1969.

D6 *The Young American Poets*. Paul Caroll, ed. Chicago: Big Table-Follett, 1968. *Contains*: "Apparitions Are Not Singular Occurrences," "Belly Dancer," "A Child, a Wasp, and an Apricot Tree," "Follow That Stagecoach," "George Washington Absent from His Country," "Sometimes Even My Knees Smile," "To Celebrate My Body."

D7 *The Contemporary American Poets: American Poetry Since 1940*. Mark Strand, ed. New York: Meridian, 1969. *Contains*: "Inside Out."

D8   *Mad Windows*. Paul Perry, ed. Notre Dame, Indiana: Lit Press, 1969. *Contains*: "The Universes."

D9   *The New Yorker Book of Poems: Selected by the Editors of The New Yorker*. New York: Viking, 1969. *Contains*: "Inside Out."

D10   *Doctor Generosity's Almanac: 17 Poets*. Ray Freed, ed. New York: Doctor Generosity Press, 1970. *Contains*: "Sister Diane's Book of the Zodiac."

D11   *Inside Outer Space; New Poems of the Space Age*. Robert Vas Dias, ed. New York: Anchor-Doubleday, 1970. *Contains*: "The Moon Has a Complicated Geography."

D12   *The Voice That Is Great Within Us: American Poetry of the Twentieth Century*. Hayden Carruth, ed. New York: Bantam, 1970. *Contains*: "Patriotic Poem," "The Night a Sailor Came to Me in a Dream," "Summer."

D13   *A Caterpillar Anthology*. Clayton Eshleman, ed. New York: Anchor-Doubleday, 1971. *Contains*: "Lament of the Lady Bank Dick," "I Have Had to Learn to Live with My Face."

D14   *The College Anthology of British and American Poetry*. A. Kent Hieatt and William Park, eds. 2nd ed. Newton, Massachusetts: Allyn, 1972. *Contains*: "Rain Trip," "Sestina from the Home Gardener."

D15   *Equal Time*. Hugh Seidman and Frances Whyatt, eds. New York: Equal Time Press, 1972. *Contains*: "To a Friend Who Cannot Accept My Judgment of Him."

D16   *An Introduction to Poetry*. Louis Simpson, ed. 2nd ed. New York: St. Martin's, 1972. *Contains*: "The Ice Eagle."

D17   *Beginnings in Poetry*. William J. Martz, ed. 2nd ed. Glenview, Illinois: Scott, 1973. *Contains*: "Fire Island Poem," "Love Letter Postmarked Van Beethoven."

D18   *Contemporary Poetry in America*. Miller Williams, ed. New York: Random House, 1973. *Contains*: "Love to My Electric Handmixer," "Thank You for the Valentine."

D19   *Loves, Etc*. Marguerite Harris, ed. New York: Anchor-Doubleday, 1973. *Contains*: "The Realization of Difference."

D20   *Messages: A Thematic Anthology of Poetry*. X.J. Kennedy, ed. Boston: Little, Brown, 1973. *Contains*: "Anticipation of Sharks."

D21   *Modern Poems: An Introduction to Poetry*. Richard Ellmann and Robert O'Clair, eds. New York: Norton, 1973. *Contains*: "Sestina from the Home Gardener," "You, Letting the Trees Stand as My Betrayer."

D22   *The Norton Anthology of Modern Poetry*. Richard Ellmann and Robert O'Clair, eds. New York: Norton, 1973. *Contains*: "Sestina from the Home Gardener," "The Turtle," "You, Letting the Trees Stand as My Betrayer."

D23   *The Norton Introduction to Literature; Combined Shorter Edition*. Carl Bain, Jerome Beaty, and J. Paul Hunter, eds. New York: Norton, 1973. *Contains*: "The Buddha Inherits 6 Cars on His Birthday."

D24   *Open Poetry: Four Anthologies of Expanded Poems*. Ronald Gross and George Quasha, eds. New York: Simon, 1973. *Contains*: "Blue Monday," "The Prince of Darkness Passing through This House," "I Have Had to Learn to Live with My Face."

D25   *Poetry (The Norton Introduction to Literature)*. J. Paul Hunter, ed. New York: Norton, 1973. *Contains*: "A Poet Recognizing the Echo of the Voice," "The Buddha Inherits 6 Cars on His Birthday."

D26   *Psyche: The Feminine Poetic Consciousness*. Barbara Segnitz and Carol Rainey, eds. New York: Dell, 1973. *Contains*: "In Gratitude to Beethoven," "In Place of a Phone Call to Arabia," "The Magician," "A Poet Recognizing the Echo of the Voice."

D27   *Shake the Kaleidoscope: A New Anthology of Modern Poetry*. Milton Klonsky, ed. New York: Pocket Books, 1973. *Contains*: "The Night a Sailor Came to Me in a Dream."

D28   *Sparrow 1–12*. Los Angeles: Black Sparrow Press, 1973. *Contains*: "Form Is an Extension of Content."

D29   *Visions of America by the Poets of Our Time*. David Kherdian, ed. New York: Macmillan, 1973. *Contains*: "Sun."

D30   *A Casebook on Anaïs Nin*. Robert Zaller, ed. New York: New American Library, 1974. *Contains*: "A Tribute to Anaïs Nin."

D31   *The Contemporary Literary Scene 1973*. Frank N. Magill, ed. Englewood Cliffs, New Jersey: Salem Press, 1974. *Contains*: "Poetry as the Dialogue We All Hope Someone Is Listening To."

D32   *The Craft of Poetry: Interviews from The New York Quarterly*. William
Packard, ed. New York: Doubleday, 1974. *Contains*: "Craft Interview with
Diane Wakoski."

D33   *Oracle, A Voluntary of Poems and Prints*. Bruce McGrew and Andrew
Rush, eds. Oracle, Arizona: Oracle Press, 1974. *Contains*: "Screw, A
Technical Love Poem." Note: A Drawing by Margaret Doogan, done
espccially for the DW poem, appears on p. [25]. Very few copies of this book
were printed. Margaret Doogan also made an animated, five minute film of
the poem.

D34   *Poetry: Points of Departure*. Henry Taylor, ed. Cambridge: Win-
throp, 1974. *Contains*: "What I Want in a Husband Besides a Mustache."

D35   *Preferences; 51 American Poets Choose Poems from Their Own Work and
from the Past*. Richard Howard, ed. New York: Viking, 1974. *Contains*:
"Ringless" (which DW has paired with Shakespeare's "Sonnet XXIX").

D36   *Search the Silence: Poems of Self-Discovery*. Betsy Ryan, ed. New York:
Scholastic, 1974. *Contains*: "Inside Out."

D37   *7 Poets 7 Poems*. Linda Lutes, ed. Providence, R.I.: Burning Deck
Press, 1974. *Contains*: "The Liar."

D38   *Sparrow 13–24*. Los Angeles: Black Sparrow Press, 1974. *Contains*:
"Dear Michael," "Whistling," "Telling You True about My Fantasy Life,"
"Discovering Michael as the King of Spain," "Touching the King of Spain
under Water," "In Praise of Modern Times."

D39   *The American Poetry Anthology*. Daniel Halpern, ed. New York:
Avon, 1975. *Contains*: "Justice Is Reason Enough," "The Mechanic,"
"Smudging," "Wind Secrets."

D40   *How Does a Poem Mean?* John Ciardi and Miller Williams, eds. 2nd
ed. Boston: Houghton, 1975. *Contains*: "Thank You for the Valentine."

D41   *O Frabjous Day! Poetry for Holidays and Special Occasions*. Myra Cohn
Livingston, ed. New York: Atheneum, 1975. *Contains*: "Patriotic Poem."

D42   *Sparrow 25–36*. Los Angeles: Black Sparrow Press, 1975. *Contains*:
"Creating a Personal Mythology."

D43   *Along Amid All This Noise: A Collection of Women's Poetry*. Ann Reit,
ed. New York: Four Winds Press, 1976. *Contains*: "The Blackbird."

D44   *CAPSton: Poems by CAPS Poetry Fellows 1970–1975*. Darcy Ryser and Bruce Benderson, eds. New York: Publishing Center for Cultural Resources, 1976. *Contains*: "Smudging."

D45   *Contemporary American and Australian Poetry*. Thomas Shapcott, ed. Queensland, Australia: U of Queensland P, 1976. *Contains*: "Children Visit the Island," "The Duchess Potatoes," "My Knees Go before the Firing Squad at Dawn," "My Mother Tries to Visit Me in the Dead of Night," "Overweight Poem," "To Bed."

D46   *The Face of Poetry*. La Verne Harrell Clark and Mary MacArthur, eds. Arlington: Gallimaufry, 1976. *Contains*: "I Have Had to Learn to Live with My Face."

D47   *I Hear My Sisters Saying: Poems by Twentieth-Century Women*. Carol Konek and Dorothy Walters, eds. New York: Crowell, 1976. *Contains*: "Journey," "No More Soft Talk."

D48   *Introducing Poems*. Linda Wagner and C. David Mead, eds. New York: Harper, 1976. *Contains*: "Summer."

D49   *Understanding Poetry*. Cleanth Brooks and Robert Penn Warren, eds. 4th ed. New York: Holt, 1976. *Contains*: "Placing a \$2 Bet for a Man Who Will Never Go to the Horse Races Any More."

D50   *The Other Side of a Poem*. Barbara Abercrombie, ed. New York: Harper, 1977. *Contains*: "I Walk the Purple Carpet into Your Eye."

D51   *Sparrow 49–60*. Santa Barbara, California: Black Sparrow Press, 1977. *Contains*: "Variations on a Theme (An Essay on Revision)."

D52   *Fine Frenzy: Enduring Themes in Poetry*. Robert Baylor and Brenda Stokes, eds. New York: McGraw-Hill, 1978. *Contains*: "No More Soft Talk."

D53   *The Poetry Anthology*. Daryl Hine and Joseph Parisi, eds. Boston: Houghton, 1978. *Contains*: "The Ring."

D54   *Sparrow 61–72*. Santa Barbara, California: Black Sparrow Press, 1978. *Contains*: "Pachelbel's Canon."

D55   *Tangled Vines: A Collection of Mother and Daughter Poems*. Lyn Lifshin, ed. Boston: Beacon Press, 1978. *Contains*: "My Mother Tries to Visit Me in the Dead of Night."

D56   *The Treasury of American Poetry*. Nancy Sullivan, ed. New York: Doubleday, 1978. *Contains*: "The Night a Sailor Came to Me in a Dream," "The Father of My Country," "An Apology."

D57   *Cody's Calendar of Contemporary Poets*. Alan Soldofsky, ed. Photographs by Joey Tranchina. Berkeley: Cody's Books, 1979. *Contains*: "Lady's Slipper."

D58   *A Geography of Poets: An Anthology of the New Poetry*. Edward Field, ed. New York: Bantam, 1979. *Contains*: "Ode to a Lebanese Crock of Olives."

D59   *In Her Own Image: Women Working in the Arts*. Elaine Hedges and Ingrid Wendt, eds. New York: Feminist Press-McGraw-Hill, 1980. *Contains*: "Medieval Tapestry and Questions."

D60   *The Poet's Choice*. George E. Murphy, Jr., ed. Green Harbor, Massachusetts: Tendril, 1980. *Contains*: "My Mother's Milkman."

D61   *Anthology of Magazine Verse and Yearbook of American Poetry 1981*. Alan F. Pater, ed. Beverly Hills, California: Monitor Book Company, 1981. *Contains*: "Aging."

D62   *From A to Z: 200 Contemporary Poets*. David Ray, ed. Athens, Ohio: Swallow Press, 1981. *Contains*: "For a Man Who Learned to Swim When He Was Sixty."

D63   *The Norton Introduction to Poetry*. J. Paul Hunter, ed. 2nd ed. New York: Norton, 1981. *Contains*: "Belly Dancer," "A Poet Recognizing the Echo of the Voice," "The Photos," "Uneasy Rider." Note: The 3rd edition includes the same poems.

D64   *Family Violence: Poems on the Pathology*. Mary McAnally, ed. La Jolla, California: Moonlight Publications, 1982. *Contains*: "Wind Secrets."

D65   *A Book to Write Poems By*. Rory Harris and Peter McFarlane, eds. Australia: Australian Association for the Teaching of English, 1983. *Contains*: "Chant for a Sharp Knife."

D66   *The Heath Guide to Poetry*. David Bergman and Daniel Epstein, eds. Lexington, Massachusetts: Heath, 1983. *Contains*: "I Have Had to Learn to Live with My Face."

D67   *Outlooks and Insights: A Reader for Writers*. Paul Eschholz and Alfred Rosa, eds. New York: St. Martin's, 1983. *Contains*: "Ode to a Lebanese Crock of Olives."

D68   *Reading and Writing Poetry: Successful Approaches for the Student and Teacher*. Charles Duke and Sally Jacobson, eds. Phoenix: Oryx Press, 1983. *Contains*: "Color Is a Poet's Tool."

D69   *Writing Poetry*. Barbara Drake. New York: Harcourt, 1983. *Contains*: "Wind Secrets," "Ode to a Lebanese Crock of Olives," "Sour Milk," "The Father of My Country."

D70   *Chelsea Retrospective, 1958–1983*. Sonia Raiziss, ed. New York: Chelsea Associates, 1984. *Contains*: "Screw, a Technical Love Poem."

D71   *Contemporary Authors; Autobiography Series*. Vol. 1. Dedria Bryfonski, ed. Detroit: Gale Research Company, 1984. *Contains*: "Diane Wakoski." Note: This is a 15,000 word autobiography, with photographs and bibliography.

D72   *The Heath Guide to Literature*. David Bergman and Daniel Mark Epstein, eds. Lexington, Massachusetts: Heath, 1984. *Contains*: "I Have Had to Learn to Live with My Face."

D73   *Inward Journey: Ross Macdonald*. Ralph B. Sipper, ed. Santa Barbara, California: Cordelia Editions, 1984. *Contains*: "George Washington and Lew Archer in the Desert."

D74   *School's Out—Now What?* Joan M. Bergstrom, ed. Berkeley: Ten Speed Press, 1984. *Contains*: "Thanking My Mother for Piano Lessons."

D75   *Tarot for Your Self*. Mary Greer, ed. Hollywood: Newcastle, 1984. *Contains*: "Poem on a Card," "The Empress # 8."

D76   *Gathered Waters: An Anthology of River Poems*. Cort Conley, ed. Cambridge, Idaho: Beckeddy Books, 1985. *Contains*: "The Canoer."

D77   *The Norton Anthology of Literature by Women: The Tradition in English*. Sandra Gilbert and Susan Gubar, eds. New York: Norton, 1985. *Contains*: "Belly Dancer," "Blue Monday," "Ringless," "My Trouble," "The Mirror of a Day Chiming Marigold."

D78   *Resist Much, Obey Little: Some Notes on Edward Abbey*. James Hepworth and Gregory McNamee, eds. Salt Lake City: Dream Garden Press, 1985. *Contains*: "Edward Abbey: Joining the Visionary 'Inhumanists.'"

D79   *Songs from Unsung Worlds*. Bonnie Bilyeu Gordon, ed. Boston: Birkhäuser, 1985. *Contains*: "For Whitman."

E. Translations

E1 "The Tightrope Walker," *Spektrum* 20 (September 1963): 12. Translated into German.

E2 "Sun," "The Sun," *El Corno Emplumado* 11 (July 1964): 7-9. Translated into Spanish, with English originals on facing pages.

E3 "Slicing Oranges for Jeremiah," *Haravec* 3 (July 1967): 59-61. Translated into Spanish by C.A. de Lomellini.

E4 "Picture of a Girl Drawn in Black and White," "The Man Who Paints Mountains," "A Child, a Wasp, and an Apricot Tree," *Revista de Bellas Artes* 23 (September–October 1968): 44-46. Translated into Spanish by Isabel Fraire.

E5 "Patriotic Poem," "You, Letting the Trees Stand as My Betrayer." *Americke Poezije.* Antun Soljan, ed. Zagreb: Nakladni Zarod Mitice Hrvatske, 1980. Translated into Serbo-Croatian.

E6 *Magellanic Clouds.* (see photo page 113.) Translated into Romanian by Liliana Ursu. Bucharest: Universe Editions, 1981. Note: This is not a translation of the American edition of *The Magellanic Clouds*. This is a selection of Wakoski poems from *The Magellanic Clouds, Smudging, Dancing on the Grave of a Son of a Bitch*, and *Trilogy*.

E7 "The Father of My Country." *TRIP: Vodic Kroz Savremenu Americku Poeziju.* V. Bajac and V. Kopicl, eds. Belgrad: Biblioteka Grifon, 1982. Translated into Serbo-Croatian.

E8 "Light," "Grey Sea," *La Mer* 7 (Summer 1983). Translated into Japanese.

Book cover of the Romanian Magellanic Clouds.

F. Published Interviews

F1 "Diane Wakoski Raps: An Interview," *Jeopardy* 6 (March 1970): 3–8.

F2 "A Terrible War: A Conversation with Diane Wakoski." With Stephen Bird and Gregory Fitz Gerald. *The Far Point* 4 (Spring–Summer 1970): 44–54. Rpt. under the same title: Philip Gerber and Robert Gemmett, eds. Winnipeg: U of Manitoba Press, 1970. Note: an offprint of the original publication, so noted on the cover, appeared from the Far Point Press, Brockport, New York, 1970, in wrappers.

F3 "The Poet Places Herself: An Interview with Diane Wakoski." With W.A. Blais. *The Falcon* 2–3 (Spring 1971): 43–52.

F4 *Comment! with Edwin Newman.* Prod. Pamela Hill. With Patricia Elliott, Robert Ardrey, Eleanor Holmes Norton, and Leslie Fiedler. NBC. 28 May 1972. *Merkle Press* 2.16.

F5 "Part I of an Interview with Diane Wakoski." With Steve Crowe. *The Penny Dreadful* 1.1 (1972): 3.

F6 "Part II of an Interview with Diane Wakoski." With Steve Crowe. *The Penny Dreadful* 1.2 (May 1972): 10–11.

F7 "Craft Interview with Diane Wakoski." With Mary Jane Fortunato. *The Craft of Poetry; Interviews from the New York Quarterly.* Ed. William Packard. New York: Doubleday, 1974. 321–340.

F8 "Death on the Nile: An Interview with Diane Wakoski." With Dan Ilves and Rick Smith. *Stonecloud* 5 (1975): 23–38.

F9 "Interview with Diane Wakoski." With Allan Goya. *Whitman College Pioneer* 84.12 (2 December 1976): 4–6. See also A57.

F10   "A Conversation with Diane Wakoski." With Larry Smith. *Chicago Review* 29.1 (1977): 115–125. Rpt. as "Diane Wakoski Interviewed by Lawrence Smith." *American Poetry Observed: Poets on Their Work*. Ed. Joe David Bellamy. Chicago: U of Illinois P, 1984. 275–284. See also A57.

F11   "An Interview with Diane Wakoski." With Elaine H. Baruch. *Pulp* 3.2–3 (1977): 10–13. See also A57.

F12   "An Interview with Diane Wakoski." With Claire Healey. *Contemporary Literature* 18 (Winter 1977): 1–19. See also A57.

F13   "A Colloquy with Diane Wakoski," *Gypsy Scholar* 6.2 (Summer 1979): 61–73.

F14   "An Interview by Taffy Martin with Diane Wakoski," *Dalhousie Review* 61.3 (Autumn 1981): 476–496.

F15   "CA Interview." With Jean W. Ross. *Contemporary Authors*. New Revision Series. Eds. Ann Evory and Linda Metzger. Vol. 9. Detroit: Gale Research Company, 1983. 511–514. Note: DW was interviewed on 15 December 1981.

F16   "Diane Wakoski." *Finding the Words: Conversations with Writers Who Teach*. By Nancy Bunge. Athens, Ohio: Swallow Press, 1985. 128–144.

Appendix:
Reviews and Criticism

AP1   Baxter, Charles. Rev. of *Inside the Blood Factory. Minnesota Review* 9.1 (1969): 77–79. "...a hypnotic style and a really bizarre personal history."

AP2   Beis, Patricia S. "Cold Fire: Some Contemporary American Women Poets." *DAI* 34 (1974): 5157A. St. Louis.

AP3   Benig, Irving. Rev. of *Greed, Parts 8, 9, 11. Library Journal* 98 (1 October 1973): 2864. "Searing, frightening poems, totally individual."

AP4   Blazek, Douglas. "Falling into Triteness." Rev. of *Smudging. Poetry* 124.3 (June 1976): 167–178. "Diane Wakoski's poems come close to being terrible; some are almost soap operas, others the grotesque fantasies of some overly imaginative and under-experienced little girl. They're self-indulgent almost to the point of obsession, over-blown almost to the point of being naive and foolish.... She is saved. Her poems are saved. This inordinate degree of intelligence, both in what she says and how she handles her poems, not only saves but is the guiding force that makes her best poems more total, more liveable, more penetrable, with more results than those written by so many of our more dichotomized poets."

AP5   Blazek, Douglas. Rev. of *Greed, Parts One and Two. The Book Review* 13 (August 1970): 20.

AP6   Bonner, Mike. "Blow Review." Rev. of *The Collected Greed. Blow* 7 (1985): 21.

AP7   Bromwich, D. Rev. of *Waiting for the King of Spain. Hudson Review* 30 (Summer 1977): 279–292.

AP8   Brook, Donna, Rev. of *Toward a New Poetry* and *Cap of Darkness. American Book Review* 3.6 (November–December 1981): 11. "Increasingly, publishing Diane Wakoski seems to be an activity with a logic and momentum all its own, for it is hard to establish a necessity for these two books."

AP9   Brown, Rosellen. "Plentitude and Dearth." *Parnassus* 1.2 (1973): 42–59. "...like some friend of yours who's flung herself down in your kitchen to tell you something urgent and makes you laugh and respect her good old-fashioned guts at the same time."

AP10   Burns, G. Rev. of *The Man Who Shook Hands. Southwest Review* 63 (Summer 1978): 303–305.

AP11   Carpenter, John E. "Revalues." Rev. of *The Magellanic Clouds. Poetry* 120.3 (June 1972): 164–169. "Her desires are open, liberal, attractive, and spendthrift; she has a marvellous desire to encompass everything."

AP12   Christensen, Paul. Rev. of *Cap of Darkness* and *The Magician's Feastletters. Sulfur* 7 (1983): 175–180. "I regard her as the ablest chronicler of a generation that has seen most of the wars and collapses of the nation in this century, and who has watched the sexual revolution redefine family, work, sexual identity, marriage, and old age. The only other poet who can match her voluminous journal-poetry is Allen Ginsberg, and together they have written the emotional history of modern America."

AP13   Rev. of *The Collected Greed. Chicago* 34 (March 1985): 113.

AP14   Rev. of *Discrepancies and Apparitions. Beloit Poetry Journal* 16.4 (Summer 1966): 39.

AP15   Rev. of *Discrepancies and Apparitions. Virginia Quarterly Review* 42 (Summer 1966): xcviii. "Sounding like a hybrid of John Ashbery, Kenneth Koch, Arnold Weinstein, and Elizabeth Bishop, if you can imagine, Miss Wakoski is often a very imaginative and lively poet of real freshness, and as often a very fake imitation of a pop art exhibition."

AP16   Earnshaw, D. Rev. of *Toward a New Poetry. World Literature Today* 55 (Spring 1981): 327. "Her critical judgment is professional. . . [but] in spite of the sound doctrines put forth here, many readers will be exasperated by the aggressive narcissism."

AP17   Enslin, Theodore. Rev. of *Inside the Blood Factory. Maps* 3 (1968): 89–90. "Superb."

AP18   Eshleman, Clayton. "Letter." *American Poetry* 2.2 (Winter 1985): 79–82. Note: This is a response to DW's essay in *American Poetry* 1.3 [see C264].

AP19   Eshleman, Clayton. "Letter." *Contemporary Literature* 16.4 (Autumn 1975): 516–527. Note: This is a reply to Marjorie G. Perloff's "The Corn-Porn Lyric: Poetry 1972–1973," in *Contemporary Literature* 16.1 [see AP62]. There is a reply to Eshleman by Perloff on pp. 527–530. The editor, L.S. Dembo, replies to Eshleman on p. 530.

AP20   Ferrier, Carole. "Sexual Politics in Diane Wakoski's Poetry." Rev. of *Virtuoso Literature. Hecate* 1.2 (July 1975): 89–94. Note: This is a strong, feminist attack on DW.

AP21   Ford, Gena. Rev. of *Coins & Coffins. Elizabeth* 6 (October 1963): 16.

AP22   Fraser, G.S. Rev. of *Trilogy. Partisan Review* 45.1 (1978): 151–157.

AP23   Gabelnick, Faith. "Making Connections: American Women Poets on Love." *DAI* 35 (1974): 2266A. American U.

AP24   Gannon, Catherine, and Clayton Lein. "Diane Wakoski and the Language of Self." *San Jose Studies* 5.2 (1979): 84–98.

AP25   Gilbert, Sandra M. "A Platoon of Poets." Rev. of *Dancing on the Grave of a Son of a Bitch. Poetry* 128.5 (August 1976): 290–299. "In choosing to write fairy tales about her secret self, Wakoski has always, of course, flirted with a little girl cuteness that threatens not to wear well, threatens to cloy as though the poet had decided to spend her life in an Alice in Wonderland costume wandering among not archetypes but stereotypes. . . . And yet perhaps these problematically weary pieces are simply signs that Wakoski—serenely established, like Koch, in the town of her career—has entered a transitional stage."

AP26   Rev. of *Greed: Parts 8, 9, 11. Choice* 10 (December 1973): 1555. "Greed, when completed, will be a major poetic achievement."

AP27   Rev. of *Greed: Parts 8, 9, 11. Virginia Quarterly Review* 49 (Autumn 1973): cxl. "The trouble is that the vanity of the speaker who is pragmatic and sophomoric by turns, sucks the air out of the room."

AP28   Hannigan, Paul. "A Word about Diane Wakoski." *Sumac* 2.1 (Fall 1969): 141–142. ". . . it is her practice to publish her poems very often in places so obscure that neither moth nor rust has heard of them."

AP29   Hitchcock, G. Rev. of *Trilogy. Western Humanities Review* 28 (Autumn 1974): 406–407.

AP30   Rev. of *Inside the Blood Factory. Virginia Quarterly Review* 45 (Summer 1969): xciii.

AP31   Jacobs, Willis D. Rev. of *Coins & Coffins* and *Four Young Lady Poets. New Mexico Quarterly* 33.4 (1964): 478–479.

AP32   Jaidka, Manju. "Sentimental Violence: A Note on Diane Wakoski and Sylvia Plath." *Notes on Contemporary Literature* 14.5 (November 1984): 2. Note: Discusses *Dancing on the Grave of a Son of a Bitch* and Plath's "Daddy."

AP33   Jeffrey, Phillis Jane Rienstra. "Diane Wakoski: An Expressive Voice in Contemporary American Poetry." *DAI* 37 (1977): 7405A–06A. U of Michigan.

AP34   Katz, Bill. Rev. of *Inside the Blood Factory. Library Journal* 93 (15 November 1968): 4301.

AP35   Kowler, Andrea. Rev. of *Waiting for the King of Spain. Library Journal* 102 (15 March 1977): 713.

AP36   Krawczyk-Smith, Maureen. "Diane Wakoski: An Annotated Bibliography of Secondary Materials." Master's thesis. Virginia Polytechnic Institute and State University, 1977. Note: This is a completely unreliable bibliography.

AP37   Lauter, Estella. "Diane Wakoski: Disentangling the Woman from the Moon." *Women as Mythmakers: Poetry and Visual Art by Twentieth-Century Women.* Bloomington: Indiana UP, 1984. 98–113. ". . . by tracing the contours of her relationship with the moon through eight books of poems, I want to explore here some of the attitudes twentieth-century women might take toward nature."

AP38   Lewis, Harry. Rev. of *The Motorcycle Betrayal Poems. Mulch* 2.2 (Winter 1973–1974): 147–150. "But finally I find that this book fails to make it."

AP39   Lutz, Kerry L. "Wakoski, Diane." *Contemporary Authors.* New Revision Series. Eds. Ann Evory and Linda Metzger. Vol. 9. Detroit: Gale Research Company, 1983. 509–511. Notes: This is a "sketch" of the poet and her work. The Lutz bibliography has two incorrect entries. "*Poems*, Key Printing Co., 1969," is a misidentification of *Odda Tala* 3. "*Some Black Poems for the Buddha's Birthday*, Pierripont Press, 1969," was never published. It was in galley proofs when the Pierripont Press failed.

AP40   Rev. of *The Magician's Feastletters. Library Journal* 107 (June 1982): 1100.

AP41   Malkoff, Karl. *Crowell's Handbook of Contemporary American Poetry.* New York: Crowell, 1973. 317–319. "She is not uniformly successful. But when she is on the mark, she is a powerful, even a terrifying, poet."

AP42   Rev. of *The Man Who Shook Hands. Choice* 15 (October 1978): 1054.

AP43   Marlatt, Daphne. Rev. of *The Magellanic Clouds. Tuatara* 3 (November 1970): 45–47.

AP44   Martin, Taffy Wynne. "Diane Wakoski's Personal Mythology: Dionysian Music, Created Presence." *Boundary* 10.3 (Spring 1982): 155–172.

AP45   Martz, L.L. Rev. of *Inside the Blood Factory. Yale Review* 58 (June 1969): 603.

AP46   Matthews, William. Rev. of *The George Washington Poems, Greed, Parts One and Two,* and *Inside the Blood Factory. Lillabulero* 7 (Summer–Fall 1969): 87–93. "Anybody who really cares about poetry should read it."

AP47   McClatchy, J.D. Rev. of *Virtuoso Literature for Two and Four Hands. Yale Review* 65 (Autumn 1975): 95. "Her intelligence is at best derivative or simplistic."

AP48   McCloud, Nedra Krishna. Rev. of *The Motorcycle Betrayal Poems. Stone Drum* 1.1 (Spring 1972): 62. "Would someone else care to be as honest?"

AP49   Meinke, Peter. Rev. of *Virtuoso Literature for Two and Four Hands. New Republic* 172 (14 June 1975): 25. "Her statements about life are not remarkable, but many of these poems and parts of poems are, especially when she sticks to the visual and informative."

AP50   Mersmann, James F. "Blood on the Moon: Diane Wakoski's Mythologies of Loss and Need." *Margins* January –February–March 1976: 116–128.

AP51   Mojtabai, A.G. Rev. of *The Motorcycle Betrayal Poems. Library Journal* 96 (15 December 1971): 4098. "It's nag, nag, nag."

AP52   Morehouse, Val. Rev. of *The Man Who Shook Hands. Library Journal* 103 (1 April 1978): 757.

AP53   Rev. of *The Motorcycle Betrayal Poems. Choice* 9 (July –August 1972): 649. ". . . among the most talented young poets of the day. Her poems are fresh and moving because they represent a very personal, and in some ways unique, expression of an individual searching to find touchstones in a world she finds confused and misdirected."

AP54   Rev. of *The Motorcycle Betrayal Poems. Virginia Quarterly Review* 48 (Autumn 1972): cxxiv.

AP55   Mottram, Eric. Rev. of *The Motorcycle Betrayal Poems. Parnassus* 1.1 (Fall–Winter 1972): 152–162. ". . . operates in a world of women as adjuncts to men and the erotics of bikes; the poems are survival gestures."

AP56   Oates, Joyce Carol. "A Cluster of Feelings: Wakoski & Levine." *American Poetry Review* 2.3 (May–June 1973): 55. Note: Reviews *Smudging*, but is also an overview of DW's poetry.

AP57   Olson, Toby, editor. "A Symposium on Diane Wakoski." *Margins* 28–29–30 (1976): 90–129. Note: Contains articles by Dave Smith, Gloria Bowles, Michael Rossman, Theodore Enslin, Rochelle Owens, William E. Thompson, Andrea Musher, Carole Ferrier, Armand Schwerner, David Ignatow, George Economou, Louis Rowan, and James F. Mersmann. Gloria Bowles: "Repetition has become Wakoski's basic stylistic mode. And since form is an extension of content (et vice versa) Wakoski's poetric themes have become obsessive. Repetition is a formal fact of her poetry and, so she suggests, the basic structure of our lives." David Ignatow: "Diane's style of writing reminds me of the baroque style of dress . . . the huge flounces, furbelows, puffed sleeves, trailing skirts, tight waist, heaving bosoms and stylishly protruding buttocks, all carried off with great elegance of movement and poise." James F. Mersmann: "I am convinced that Wakoski's poetry is a much wiser and more powerful statement about the experience of life in the 1960s and 1970s than most readers have realized."

AP58   Ostriker, Alicia. "Body Language: Imagery of the Body in Women's Poetry." *The State of the Language.* Eds. Leonard Michaels and Christopher Ricks. Berkeley: U of California P, 1980. 247–263. Note: Discusses Suckenick, Plath, Sexton, and DW.

AP59   Ostriker, Alicia. "In Mind: The Divided Self and Women's Poetry." *Midwest Quarterly* 24.4 (Summer 1983): 351–356. Note: Discusses Denise Levertov, Sylvia Plath, and DW.

AP60   Ostriker, Alicia. *Stealing the Language: The Emergence of Women's Poetry in America.* Boston: Beacon, 1986. *Passim.*

AP61   Ostriker, Alicia. "'What Are Patterns For?' Anger and Polarization in Women's Poetry." *Feminist Studies* 10.3 (Fall 1984): 485–503. Note: Discusses *The George Washington Poems* and work by Anne Sexton and Margaret Atwood.

AP62   Perloff, Marjorie G. "The Corn-Porn Lyric: Poetry 1972–1973." *Contemporary Literature* 16.1 (Winter 1975): 84–125. Note: This essay attacks DW, Robert Creeley, Charles Wright, Clayton Eshleman, Marge Piercey, and Erica Jong. "Here is Corn-Porn with a vengeance: the hard-boiled, successful girl poet who runs around with stray truckdrivers or motorcyclists, really has a heart of pure gold. . ." [see AP19].

AP63   Pritchard, William H. "Despairing at Styles." Rev. of *Virtuoso Literature for Two and Four Hands. Poetry* 127.5 (February 1976): 292–302. "It is as if

Eliot and Frost had never lived or written, and, shaking my head ruefully, I can only say that Diane Wakoski is all right if you like that sort of thing."

AP64 Regan, Robert. Rev. of *Discrepancies and Apparitions. Library Journal* 91 (1 March 1966): 1231.

AP65 Sadoff, Diane F. "Mythopoeia, the Moon and Contemporary Women's Poetry." *Massachusetts Review* 19.1 (Spring 1978): 93–110.

AP66 Sasso, Louis. Rev. of *Virtuoso Literature for Two and Four Hands. Library Journal* 100 (1 May 1975): 858.

AP67 Schjeldahl, Peter. Rev. of *The Man Who Shook Hands. N.Y. Times Book Review* 13 August 1978: 15. ". . . their pervasive unpleasantness makes her popularity rather surprising."

AP68 Slavitt, David R. "Broads." *The Brand-X Anthology of Poetry; Burnt Norton Edition.* Ed. William Zaranka. Cambridge, Massachusetts: Apple-Wood Books, 1981. Note: This is a parody.

AP69 Smith, David R. Rev. of *Cap of Darkness. Sulfur* 1 (1981): 247–254. "Such a poem and the others I have mentioned outweigh the dross, and by a good bit."

AP70 Spector, R.D. Rev. of *Inside the Blood Factory. Saturday Review* 52 (15 March 1969): 33. "Miss Wakoski's social comment is ruthless. . . . To speak of liking Miss Wakoski's poetry would seem inappropriate; to deny it full admiration would be dishonest."

AP71 Stern, Frederick C. Rev. of *The Collected Greed: Parts 1–13. Chicago* 34.3 (March 1985): 113. "Its combination of fantasy and lyricism and tough-talking Americanisms is delightful, and delightfully Wakoski."

AP72 Taylor, Charles. Rev. of selections from *Greed. Big Boulevard* 3.1 (1973): 12–16.

AP73 Taylor, Mark. Rev. of *The Motorcycle Betrayal Poems. Commonweal* 97 (3 November 1972): 112.

AP74 Thayler, Carl. Letter. *Caterpillar* 5.2, no. 18 (April 1972): 122–123. Note: This letter is a reply to a DW review [see C148].

AP75 Rev. of *Toward a New Poetry. Choice* 17 (July–August 1980): 675.

AP76 Vendler, Helen. Rev. of *Virtuoso Literature for Two and Four Hands. N.Y. Times Book Review* 6 April 1975: 4. "Her biting poems on men and her touching poems on her childhood and adolescence have by now earned her a place in all the anthologies, and she has every right to pause and think about her own writing. Most of the poems here concern art, but art seems less amenable to Wakoski's discursive and meandering meditations than past anecdotes. Her descriptions here of flowers, landscapes and birds bear traces, perhaps inevitably, of Lawrence . . . but, where his language is driven and his pacing relentless, hers is nerveless and weak."

AP77 Wagner, Linda. "Poetry: The 1930s to the Present." *American Literary Scholarship.* Durham, North Carolina: Duke UP, 1977. 379–398. ". . . her vehicle is the mythology of her personal narratives."

AP78 Wagner, Linda. Rev. of *Waiting for the King of Spain. The Nation* 224.11 (19 March 1977): 348. ". . . includes impressive poems about the poet as explorer of human needs and satisfactions."

AP79 Wagner, Linda. Rev. of *Waiting for the King of Spain. Ontario Review* 7 (Fall–Winter 1977–1978): 88–95.

AP80 Wagner, Linda. "Wakoski and Rukeyser." Rev. of *Waiting for the King of Spain. American Modern: Essays in Fiction and Poetry.* Port Washington, New York: Kennikat Press, 1980. 235–237.

AP81 Wagner, Linda. "Wakoski's Poems: Moving past Confession." Rev. of *The Man Who Shook Hands. Atlantic Review* ns 2 (Autumn 1979): 60–68. "Walt Whitman would be proud."

AP82   Wah, Fredric. Rev. of *Four Young Lady Poets*. *TISH* 14 (October 1962): 6.

AP83   Rev. of *Waiting for the King of Spain*. *Choice* 14 (July–August 1977): 685.

AP84   Rev. of *Waiting for the King of Spain*. *Library Journal* 102 (15 March 1977): 713.

AP85   Waldrop, Bernard. Rev. of *Coins & Coffins*. *Burning Deck* 1 (Fall 1962): 57. "From this beginning, though the range here is not great, it seems likely that she can do anything she wants to."

AP86   Watkins, Evan. "Historical Criticism and Contemporary Poetry." *Contemporary Literature* 22.4 (Fall 1981): 556–573.

AP87   Weller, Sheila. "The Mercy and Ironies of Memory: The Poetry of Diane Wakoski." *Ms.* 4.9 (March 1976): 82–83. "At 38, Diane Wakoski is probably the most prolific young poet in America. She's also that rare poet who has never been anything but self-supporting; that rarer poet who makes a good living exclusively from her books, readings, and workshops; and that rarest of all poets who has achieved high critical esteem without sacrificing her audience, popular devotion without compromising her art."

AP88   Weller, Sheila. "The Poetess: Duel, Sigh, or Shrug?" Rev. of *The Motorcycle Betrayal Poems*. *Village Voice* 21 December 1972: 26.

AP89   Williamson, Alan. "The Future of Personal Poetry." *Introspection and Contemporary Poetry*. Cambridge, Massachusetts: Harvard UP, 1984. 149–191.

AP90   Zivkovic, P.D. Rev. of *Inside the Blood Factory*. *Southwest Review* 60 (Spring 1975): 212–216.

AP91   Zweig, Paul. Rev. of *The Motorcycle Betrayal Poems*. *N.Y. Times Book Review* 12 December 1971: 5. "She digs her teeth into the slaveries of woman, she cries them aloud with such fulminating energy that the chains begin to melt of themselves."

Title Index

C

H

I

M

N

T

Y